CIMA

Strategic Level

F3

Financial Strategy

Exam
Practice Kit

For exams from 4 November 2019 to January 2021.

Sixth edition 2019

ISBN 9781 5097 2710 0
e-ISBN 9781 5097 2760 5

British Library Cataloguing-in-Publication Data
A catalogue record for this book
is available from the British Library

Published by

BPP Learning Media Ltd
BPP House, Aldine Place, 142/144 Uxbridge Road
London W12 8AA

www.bpp.com/learningmedia

Printed in the United Kingdom

Your learning materials, published by BPP Learning Media
Ltd, are printed on paper obtained from traceable,
sustainable sources.

We are grateful to the Chartered Institute of Management
Accountants for allowing us to reproduce extracts from the
CIMA exam blueprint. An up-to-date version of the full
blueprint is available at www.cimaglobal.com/examblueprints.

A note about copyright

Dear Customer

What does the little © mean and why does it matter?

Your market-leading BPP books, course materials
and e-learning materials do not write and update
themselves. People write them: on their own behalf
or as employees of an organisation that invests in
this activity. Copyright law protects their livelihoods.
It does so by creating rights over the use of the
content.

Breach of copyright is a form of theft – as well as
being a criminal offence in some jurisdictions, it is
potentially a serious breach of professional ethics.

With current technology, things might seem a bit
hazy but, basically, without the express permission
of BPP Learning Media:

- Photocopying our materials is a breach of
  copyright

- Scanning, ripcasting or conversion of our digital
  materials into different file formats, uploading
  them to facebook or emailing them to your
  friends is a breach of copyright

You can, of course, sell your books, in the form in
which you have bought them – once you have
finished with them. (Is this fair to your fellow
students? We update for a reason.) Please note the
e-products are sold on a single user licence basis:
we do not supply 'unlock' codes to people who have
bought them second-hand.

And what about outside the UK? BPP Learning Media
strives to make our materials available at prices
students can afford by local printing arrangements,
pricing policies and partnerships which are clearly
listed on our website. A tiny minority ignore this and
indulge in criminal activity by illegally photocopying
our material or supporting organisations that do. If
they act illegally and unethically in one area, can
you really trust them?

Contents

BPP
LEARNING
MEDIA

Question and Answer index

Using your BPP Exam Practice Kit

One of the key criteria for achieving exam success is question practice. There is generally a direct correlation between candidates who study all topics and practise exam questions and those who are successful in their real exams. This Kit gives you ample opportunity for such practice throughout your preparations for your OT exam.

All questions in your exam are compulsory and all the component learning outcomes will be examined so you must **study the whole syllabus**. Selective studying will limit the number of questions you can answer and hence reduce your chances of passing. It is better to go into the exam knowing a reasonable amount about most of the syllabus rather than concentrating on a few topics to the exclusion of the rest.

Practising as many exam-style questions as possible will be the key to passing this exam. You must do questions under **timed conditions**.

Breadth of question coverage

Questions will cover the whole of the syllabus so you must study all the topics in the syllabus.

The weightings in the table below indicate the approximate proportion of study time you should spend on each topic, and is related to the number of questions per syllabus area in the exam.

F3 Financial Strategy Syllabus topics	Weighting
A Financing policy decisions	15%
B Sources of long-term funds	25%
C Financial risks	20%
D Business valuation	40%

(CIMA exam blueprint, 2019)

Examination structure

The Objective Test exam

Pass mark	70%
Format	Computer-based assessment
Duration	90 minutes
Number of questions	60
Marking	No partial marking – each question marked correct or incorrect All questions carry the same weighting (ie same marks)
Weighting	As per syllabus areas All representative task statements from the examination blueprint will be covered
Question Types	Multiple choice Multiple response Drag and drop Gap fill Hot spot
Booking availability	On demand
Results	Immediate

What the examiner means

The table below has been prepared by CIMA to further help you interpret the syllabus and learning outcomes and the meaning of questions.

You will see that there are five skills levels you may be expected to demonstrate, ranging from Remembering and Understanding to Evaluation. CIMA Certificate subjects only use levels 1 to 3, but in CIMA's Professional qualification the entire hierarchy will be used.

Skills level		Verbs used	Definition
Level 5	Evaluation *The examination or assessment of problems, and use of judgment to draw conclusions*	Advise	Counsel, inform or notify
		Assess	Evaluate or estimate the nature, ability or quality of
		Evaluate	Appraise or assess the value of
		Recommend	Propose a course of action
		Review	Assess and evaluate in order, to change if necessary
		Select	Choose an option or course of action after consideration of the alternatives

Skills level		Verbs used	Definition
Level 4	**Analysis** *The examination and study of the interrelationships of separate areas in order to identify causes and find evidence to support inferences*	Align	Arrange in an orderly way
		Analyse	Examine in detail the structure of
		Communicate	Share or exchange information
		Compare and contrast	Show the similarities and/or differences between
		Develop	Grow and expand a concept
		Discuss	Examine in detail by argument
		Examine	Inspect thoroughly
		Monitor	Observe and check the progress of
		Prioritise	Place in order of priority or sequence for action
		Produce	Create or bring into existence
Level 3	**Application** *The use or demonstration of knowledge, concepts or techniques*	Apply	Put to practical use
		Calculate	Ascertain or reckon mathematically
		Conduct	Organise and carry out
		Demonstrate	Prove with certainty or exhibit by practical means
		Determine	Ascertain or establish exactly by research or calculation
		Perform	Carry out, accomplish, or fulfil
		Prepare	Make or get ready for use
		Reconcile	Make or prove consistent/compatible
		Record	Keep a permanent account of facts, events or transactions
		Use	Apply a technique or concept

Skills level		Verbs used	Definition
Level 1/2	**Remembering and understanding** *The perception and comprehension of the significance of an area utilising knowledge gained*	Define	Give the exact meaning of
		Describe	Communicate the key features of
		Distinguish	Highlight the differences between
		Explain	Make clear or intelligible/state the meaning or purpose of
		Identify	Recognise, establish or select after consideration
		Illustrate	Use an example to describe or explain something
		List	Make a list of
		Recognise	Identify/recall
		State	Express, fully or clearly, the details/facts of
		Outline	Give a summary of
		Understand	Comprehend ideas, concepts and techniques

(CIMA exam blueprint, 2019)

How to pass

Good exam technique

The best approach to the computer-based assessment (CBA)

You're not likely to have a great deal of spare time during the CBA itself, so you must make sure you don't waste a single minute.

You should:

1. Click 'Next' for any that have long scenarios or are very complex and return to these later
2. When you reach the 60th question, use the Review Screen to return to any questions you skipped past or any you flagged for review

Here's how the tools in the exam will help you to do this in a controlled and efficient way.

The 'Next' button

What does it do? This will move you on to the next question whether or not you have completed the one you are on.

When should I use it? Use this to move through the exam on your first pass through if you encounter a question that you suspect is going to take you a long time to answer. The Review Screen (see below) will help you to return to these questions later in the exam.

The 'Flag for Review' button

What does it do? This button will turn the icon yellow and when you reach the end of the exam questions you will be told that you have flagged specific questions for review. If the exam time runs out before you have reviewed any flagged questions, they will be submitted as they are.

When should I use it? Use this when you've answered a question but you're not completely comfortable with your answer. If there is time left at the end, you can quickly come back via the Review Screen (see below), but if time runs out at least it will submit your current answer. Do not use the Flag for Review button too often or you will end up with too long a list to review at the end. Important note —studies have shown that you are usually best to stick with your first instincts!

The Review Screen

What does it do? This screen appears after you click 'Next' on the 60th question. It shows you any incomplete questions and any you have flagged for review. It allows you to jump back to specific questions **or** work through all your incomplete questions **or** work through all your flagged for review questions.

When should I use it? As soon as you've completed your first run through the exam and reached the 60th question. The very first thing to do is to work through all your incomplete questions as they will all be marked as incorrect if you don't submit an answer for these in the remaining time. Importantly, this will also help to pick up any questions you thought you'd completed but didn't answer properly (eg you only picked two answer options in a multi-response question that required three answers to be selected). After you've submitted answers for all your incomplete questions you should use the Review Screen to work through all the questions you flagged for review.

The different Objective Test question types

Passing your CBA is all about demonstrating your understanding of the technical syllabus content. You will find this easier to do if you are comfortable with the different types of Objective Test questions that you will encounter in the CBA, especially if you have a practised approach to each one.

You will find yourself continuously practising these styles of questions throughout your Objective Test programme. This way you will check and reinforce your technical knowledge at the same time as becoming more and more comfortable with your approach to each style of question.

Multiple choice

Standard multiple choice items provide four options. One option is correct and the other three are incorrect. Incorrect options will be plausible, so you should expect to have to use detailed, syllabus-specific knowledge to identify the correct answer rather than relying on common sense.

Multiple response

A multiple response item is the same as a multiple choice question, except **more than one** response is required. You will normally (but not always) be told how many options you need to select.

Drag and drop

Drag and drop questions require you to drag a 'token' onto a pre-defined area. These tokens can be images or text. This type of question is effective at testing the order of events, labelling a diagram or linking events to outcomes.

Gap fill

Gap fill (or 'fill in the blank') questions require you to type a short numerical response. You should carefully follow the instructions in the question in terms of how to type your answer – eg the correct number of decimal places.

Hot spot

These questions require you to identify an area or location on an image by clicking on it. This is commonly used to identify a specific point on a graph or diagram.

A final word on time management

Time does funny things in an exam!

Scientific studies have shown that humans have great difficulty in judging how much time has passed if they are concentrating fully on a challenging task (which your CBA should be!).

You can try this for yourself. Have a go at, say, five questions for your paper, and notice what time you start at. As soon as you finish the last question try to estimate how long it took you and then compare to your watch. The majority of us tend to underestimate how quickly time passes and this can cost you dearly in a full exam if you don't take steps to keep track of time.

So, the key thing here is to set yourself sensible milestones, and then get into the habit of regularly checking how you are doing against them:

- You need to develop an internal warning system – 'I've now spent more than three minutes on this one calculation – this is too long and I need to move on!' (less for a narrative question!)

- Keep your milestones in mind (eg approximately 30 questions done after 45 mins). If you are a distance from where you should be then adjust your pace accordingly. This usually means speeding up but can mean slowing down a bit if needs be, as you may be rushing when you don't need to and increasing the risk of making silly mistakes.

A full exam will be a mix of questions you find harder and those you find easier, and in the real CBA the order is randomised, so you could get a string of difficult questions right at the beginning of your exam. Do not be put off by this – they should be balanced later by a series of questions you find easier.

Objective test questions

1 Strategic objectives

1.1 Easycare Linens Co made a profit before interest and taxation for the year of $950,000. Net interest payable was $50,000. Tax was $100,000. In addition to a nominal issued share capital of $3m there are 1 million 10% preferred shares in issue, each with a nominal value of $1.

What is the profit figure to be used in the EPS calculation?

O $950,000

O $900,000

O $800,000

O $700,000

1.2 Anthony Inc achieved earnings per share of $0.25 and paid a dividend of $0.05 per share for the year just ended. Anthony's P/E ratio is currently 13. Its comparative data for the previous year was as follows:

EPS $0.20
DPS $0.04
P/E ratio   12.5
Dividend yield 1.6%

What total shareholder return (TSR) has Anthony achieved in the current year?

TSR is [   ] to the nearest %.

1.3 The figures in the table below are an extract from the income statement of Arnold Co. Arnold has 3.5 million ordinary shares in issue (nominal value 50 cents each) with a market price of $2.

Profit before tax $2.5 million
Less tax $0.75 million
Profit after tax $1.75 million
Ordinary dividend $0.5 million
Preference dividend $0.25 million

What is the dividend yield (to the nearest %)?

O   7%

O   4%

O   11%

O   5%

BPP
LEARNING
MEDIA

1.4 The projected income statement of SD Co for the year to 30 June 20X1 shows the following figures.

Operating profit $100,000
Interest payable $40,000
Profit before tax $60,000
Corporation tax (30%) $18,000
Profit after tax $42,000

The directors of SD Co estimate that the additional purchase of new equipment on 1 July 20X0 for $140,000 would increase the projected profit before interest and tax for the year by $18,000.

The machine would be financed by a new loan raised on 1 July 20X0 with a coupon rate of 5%.

The additional profit and interest are not reflected in the above projected income statement.

SD Co has a covenant on an existing loan stating that the interest cover must be at least 2.2.

What would be the outcome if the directors purchased the new machine?

O Interest cover is 2.95, the debt covenant is broken

O Interest cover is 2.51, the debt covenant is not broken

O Interest cover is 1.06, the debt covenant is broken

O Interest cover is 2.95, the debt covenant is not broken

1.5 **In the context of managing performance in 'not for profit' organisations, which of the following definitions is LEAST accurate?**

O Value for money means providing a service in a way which is economical, efficient and effective.

O Economy means doing things cheaply: not spending $2 when the same thing can be bought for $1.

O Efficiency means doing things quickly: minimising the amount of time that is spent on a given activity.

O Effectiveness means doing the right things: spending funds so as to achieve the organisation's objectives.

1.6 A public sector college receives government sponsorship for certain courses which are needed locally in the form of a fixed fee for each student completing such courses to a satisfactory level. The college operates within very tight budgetary cash contraints.

Which THREE of the following would be MOST important in a value for money review of this college by the government?

☐ Number of students enrolled

☐ Cost per student of providing tuition

☐ Student achievement level

☐ Student satisfaction with facilities

☐ Cash deficit avoided

1.7   Which of the following provides the BEST definition of the primary financial objective of a profit-making company?

O   To maximise the wealth of its ordinary shareholders

O   To maximise the level of annual profits

O   To achieve long term growth in earnings

O   To maximise the level of annual dividends

1.8   Entity A is a publicly listed healthcare provider and operates a number of private hospitals in Country X.

Entity B is a state-controlled and owned healthcare provider with a substantial proportion of its funding provided by the government of Country X.

Which of the following statements concerning the objectives of the two entities are correct?

Select ALL that apply.

☐   The primary objective of Entity A will be to maximise shareholder wealth.

☐   Entity A will have financial objectives but Entity B will not.

☐   Entity B will have to demonstrate value for money.

☐   The managers of Entity B are likely to have very little input or choice over its objectives.

1.9   The following is an extract from STH Co's accounts:

Turnover	$350 million
Operating costs	$125 million
Interest payable	$50 million
Taxation	$50 million
Ordinary dividends	$100 million
Shares in issue	1,000 million
Share price	300 cents

What are STH Co's earnings per share (EPS) and price–earnings (P/E) ratio?

STH Co's EPS is ☐ c (to one decimal point)

STH Co's P/E multiple is ☐ times

1.10   Company X has a 5% $200 million bank loan with a covenant that interest cover must remain above 6. Company X currently has forecast profit before tax of $81 million. Company X plans to take out a new 6% $50 million loan from a different bank (with no covenant).

If the new loan is taken out which of the following statements is true?

☐   Interest cover is 6.2 and the existing covenant will be breached

☐   Interest cover is 6.2 and the existing covenant will not be breached

☐   Interest cover is 7 and the existing covenant will be breached

☐   Interest cover is 7 and the existing covenant will not be breached

1.11   Z Supermarkets (ZS) was founded as a grocery retailer 20 years ago. It has achieved substantial growth and succeeded in gaining market share in a competitive environment. ZS is now one of the world's largest chain of stores.

ZS has the following financial objective:

- Achieve consistent growth in earnings of 8% each year.

Given the highly competitive environment in which ZS operates the board are concerned about continuing to meet their earnings growth objective. They are therefore currently evaluating a proposal to open up a new type of store called 'ZX Xpress'. These would be local convenience stores stocking mainly food with an emphasis on higher-margin products. If ZS Xpress is launched, forecast earnings for ZS over the next three years are expected to be:

	$ million
Year 1	20
Year 2	22
Year 3	25
Year 4	29
Year 5	34

What is the compound annual growth in earnings forecast for the next five years if ZS Xpress is launched?

|_____| % to the nearest whole percentage point.

1.12   Company W is a film production company based in Country W with the W$ as its currency. It has grown rapidly by acquiring other major studios as well as growing organically. It is now the largest global film making company in the world, successfully making and distributing films as well as owning an impressive library of film content.

The directors of Company W have just received the opportunity to tender for a new contract with X Net (XN), a video streaming company also located in Country W. The proposal is that W would produce films which will then be exclusively shown by XN in return for a fee set a fixed number of W$ for each W film shown. Forecast results of the first year of the contract are as follows:

	Year 1 W$'000
Revenue	2,000
Cost of sales	(1,200)
Gross profit	800
Operating expenses	(400)
Profit before interest and tax	400
Interest	(100)
Profit before tax	300
Tax @ 20%	(60)
Profit after tax	240

The following information is relevant:

- Cost of sales are a variable cost.
- Operating expenses are a fixed cost.
- Interest is based on W$2 million bank borrowings at a variable rate of 5%.

There is some uncertainty surrounding the economic environment in Country W which is causing concern for the board. Demand for the films produced under the new contract could be 10% lower than forecast and interest rates could increase to 7%.

If demand falls and interest rates increase (and all other variables stay the same) what is the expected earnings generated in Year 1 from the new contract?

○   W$144,000

○   W$176,000

○   W$48,000

○   W$240,000

1.13   A company paid the following dividend in recent years:

	20X2	20X3	20X4	20X5	20X6
Total dividend ($million)	50	55	65	90	108
Number of shares (million)	5	5	5	6	6

What is the company's compound annual growth in dividend per share since 20X2?

[   ] % to the nearest whole percentage.

1.14   AA is a car manufacturer. Its key assets are:

• Factories
• Plant and machinery
• Warehouses
• Inventory (raw materials, work in progress, finished goods)

The International Integrated Reporting Council (IIRC) has created categories of capital for inclusion where relevant in an integrated report.

Which category of capital do the above assets relate to?

○   Financial capital

○   Natural capital

○   Manufactured capital

○   Social and relationship capital

1.15   SR is a service-based entity which relies on its human resources to generate revenue.

Which THREE of the following would be potential advantages to INVESTORS if SR included voluntary narrative disclosures in respect of human capital?

☐   The market would become aware of the investment ST has made in its employees which would create greater market confidence in SR and potentially result in an increase in share price.

☐   Comprehensive disclosure would be more likely to result in an unqualified audit report.

☐   Employees would feel more valued and potentially work harder generating additional profit for SR.

☐   It would help improve staff retention and would attract potential new high quality employees to the company generating increased return for investors through retaining and recruiting talent.

☐   The time and cost of producing these disclosures would have an adverse effect on SR's profitability.

☐   It would be easier for SR to raise finance in the future.

2   Strategic financial policy decisions

2.1   **Which of the following are likely to be the main focus of financial decision-making for a company that is in the early stages of its life cycle?**

Select ALL that apply.

☐   Deciding on the level of dividend to be paid

☐   Planning and obtaining suitable sources of finance

☐   Social and environmental reporting

☐   Generating and evaluating investment proposals

2.2   Company DGG has a share price of $10 and 100 million ordinary shares in issue.

DGG has just made an announcement that a new investment idea has been assessed as having an NPV of negative $20 million.

Assume markets are efficient and information is readily available to investors.

What would be the expected effect on Company DGG's share price?

○   It will fall by 20 cents (ie $0.20) per share

○   It will rise by 20 cents (ie $0.20) per share

○   It will fall by 2 cents (ie $0.02) per share

○   No impact

2.3 Which TWO of the following statements are MOST likely to be correct in relation to the three financial management decisions?

☐ High-growth companies are likely to need high levels of capital investment, use low levels of debt finance and retain high proportions of profits rather than pay out dividends.

☐ High-growth companies are likely to need high levels of capital investment, use high levels of debt finance and retain high proportions of profits rather than pay out dividends.

☐ High-growth companies are likely to need high levels of capital investment, use low levels of debt and pay out relatively high proportions of their profits as dividends.

☐ Mature companies tend not to require high levels of capital investment, they use high levels of debt and make high dividend payouts.

☐ Mature companies tend not to require high levels of capital investment, they use low levels of debt and make high dividend payouts.

2.4 (EPS × Dividend payout %) ÷ (EPS × P/E ratio)

The above formula would generate which of the following financial indicators?

○ Cost of equity

○ Dividend cover

○ Return on equity

○ Dividend yield

2.5 Dividend yield is 6%. Earnings per share is 45 cents. Price to earnings ratio is 22.

What is the dividend per share?

○ 1.3 cents

○ 2.7 cents

○ 59.4 cents

○ 990 cents

2.6 **State whether the following statements are true or false:**

	True	False
Using a loan sourced in an overseas country can be an effective way to manage translation and political risk.	☐	☐
High-growth companies are inherently risky because of the speed of their transformation as they grow so they usually require low levels of debt and high dividend payout ratios.	☐	☐
Withholding tax increases the political risk associated with making investments overseas.	☐	☐

2.7 It is currently half way through the financial year. A toy manufacturer has produced the following forecast data for the next six-month (183 day) period to show its bank.

	$000
Sales revenue (cash sales)	17,200
Purchases (60-day credit)	8,400
Other costs (settled immediately)	8,000

In the previous six-month (183 day) period prior to the forecast the purchases were also $8,400,000 and on 60-day credit terms.

The company has an overdraft balance of $200,000. The agreed overdraft facility is $1,800,000.

Sales and purchases can be assumed to arise evenly over the period.

If all suppliers were to suddenly withdraw credit at the end of Month 6, would the overdraft facility be adequate?

○ Yes, the bank account would not be overdrawn.

○ Yes, approximately $1,020,000 of the overdraft facility would still be available for drawdown.

○ No, the overdraft facility would be exceeded by approximately $360,000.

○ No, the overdraft facility would be exceeded by approximately $2,160,000.

2.8 **Which THREE of the following strategies are MOST likely to enhance shareholder wealth?**

☐ Investment in projects with a positive Net Present Value

☐ Increasing the rate of dividend growth

☐ Enhancing brand reputation and recognition

☐ Increasing director bonuses

☐ Moving profitable operations to low-tax regimes

2.9 A company has an earnings per share ratio of 38.5 cents. It pays out 40% of its distributable profits as a dividend.

It has a price to earnings ratio of 12.

Complete the sentence below by typing in the missing information in the gaps provided.

Give your answer to one decimal place of a cent.

The company's dividend is [   ] cents per share and its share price is

[   ] cents per share.

2.10 Select the words true or false next to the following statements as appropriate.

	True	False
A company that increases its profit will always see an increase in its share price as a result.	☐	☐
A key consideration in the financing decision is to maximise the cost of capital.	☐	☐
Keeping surplus cash in order to pay a larger than usual tax liability in three months is an example of the speculative motive.	☐	☐

3 Long-term debt finance

3.1 State whether the following statements are true or false:

	True	False
Unsecured bonds are likely to require a higher yield to maturity than equivalent secured bonds.	☐	☐
Convertible bonds give the borrower the right but not the obligation to turn the bond into a predetermined number of ordinary shares.	☐	☐
A Eurobond is a bond that is denominated in a currency which is not native to where the bond itself is issued.	☐	☐

3.2 Which of the following BEST describes the term 'coupon rate' as it applies to bonds?

○   Annual interest received as a % of the ex-interest market price of the bond

○   The annual interest received as a % of the cum-interest market price of the bond

○   Annual interest received as a % of the nominal value of the bond

○   Return received taking into account capital repayment as well as interest payments

3.3 Which of the following statements in respect of convertible bonds issued by a company are either TRUE or FALSE?

	True	False
On conversion date, the ordinary shareholders of the company have the option to choose whether or not the bonds should be converted into shares.	☐	☐
The bondholder can normally claim tax relief on interest paid on the bond up to conversion.	☐	☐

3.4 **What is a dividend restraint covenant?**

    ○   An undertaking by a company to a lender to keep dividend payments within a specified limit

    ○   An undertaking by a company to its shareholders to maintain dividends at or above a specified minimum level

    ○   An undertaking by a company to a lender not to pay dividends until all outstanding interest payment obligations have been met

    ○   A restriction on dividend payments by a company due to having insufficient free cash flow

---

3.5 S is a small unlisted engineering company, established two years ago, which operates in Country S. The currency used in Country S is the S$.

S has a high level of fixed costs. S has grown rapidly over the last two years and is now looking to significantly expand its capacity by acquiring new machinery at a cost of S$2 million.

S is concerned about the state of the economy in Country S, which is highly unpredictable. The central bank in Country S has had to make a number of changes to interest rates in recent years.

If the money is borrowed, a debt covenant would be imposed on net debt to EBITDA. S regards this covenant as manageable given the current level of interest rates.

Which of the following would be the MOST appropriate source of finance for S to finance the new machinery?

    ○   A floating-rate bank loan

    ○   A lease

    ○   A revolving credit facility

    ○   A bond issue

3.6 Xpat Co is an established, unlisted, local travel agency that operates in a region of Country Y whose currency is the Y$.

Xpat is concerned with its dependence on bank finance because it is aware that banks are currently cutting back on their commercial loan portfolios, so future bank loans may be slow to obtain and expensive – if they are available at all.

Xpat is looking to raise new debt finance for a five-year period to finance the acquisition of new sites within Country Y.

Eurobonds denominated in US$ are currently trading at a low rate of interest.

Which of the following sources of finance is MOST likely to be suitable?

    ○   Convertible bond

    ○   Leasing

    ○   Eurobonds denominated in US$

    ○   Retained earnings

3.7   A 5% bond has the following characteristics:

- It is trading at $105 per $100 nominal on 1 January 20X2
- Total nominal value $200 million
- Interest is paid in arrears
- It is redeemable at par on 31 December 20X2

How much must the issuer pay to the bondholders on 31 December 20X2?

O $10 million

O $210 million

O $220 million

O $200 million

3.8   **State whether the following statements are true or false:**

	True	False
Deep discounted bonds always have a lower market value than nominal value and sometimes have a lower coupon rate than other bonds with similar risk profile.	☐	☐
For irredeemable or undated bonds the higher the issue price the higher the yield for the investor who subscribes for them.	☐	☐
Zero coupon bonds must be redeemed at par in order to give the lender an appropriate yield to maturity.	☐	☐

3.9   A listed company requires additional finance to fund various new projects. It has decided to use debt finance and considering using either a public issue or private placement of bonds.

Which of THREE of the following are advantages of using a private placement of bonds compared with a public issue?

☐   The issue costs are likely to be lower.

☐   The regulatory requirements will be less onerous.

☐   The coupon rate is likely to be lower.

☐   The funds can be raised more quickly.

☐   A larger amount of finance can be raised.

3.10   Benchmark plc has made an issue of 10% convertible bonds with a par value of $100; their market price today is $110 per $100 nominal value.

In three years time, the bonds can be redeemed at $120, or converted into shares at the rate of 50 shares per $100 bonds.

At which of the following share prices would an investor opt to take the shares?

O $2.20

O $1.50

O $2.00

O $2.50

3.11 Xyrox Co is a fast growing online marketing company. It has just submitted an application to its bank for a substantial new five-year loan.

Which of the following is likely to be LEAST important to the bank as part of its assessment of this loan?

- ○ Financial statements of Xyrox Co for the last three years.
- ○ Detailed analysis of the current management team.
- ○ An analysis of Xyrox Co's strategic plan.
- ○ Cash flow forecasts for the next five years.

3.12 H is a listed company and requires additional finance to fund a new project. The project is expected to generate low returns in the first five years, and substantial cash flows thereafter. H is considering issuing convertible bonds instead of conventional redeemable bonds.

Which of the following is the MOST likely reason for H deciding to issue convertible bonds?

- ○ Convertible bonds are treated as equity and will therefore reduce the gearing ratio.
- ○ Convertible bonds have a lower coupon rate.
- ○ Convertible bonds have a lower yield to maturity.
- ○ Convertible bonds have no redemption cost as they are converted to equity.

3.13 A business has decided to install a new machine. The machine costs $50,000 and it would have a useful life of five years with a trade-in value of $10,000 at the end of the fifth year.

The business could purchase the machine for cash, using bank loan facilities on which the current cost of debt is 9% after tax.

The rate of tax is 30% and the business will be able to claim a tax depreciation allowance of 100% in Year 1. Tax is payable with no delay.

What is the present value of the purchase costs?

$ [   ] to the nearest $100.

3.14 Electro Co has decided to lease a new machine, this would involve payment of $12,000 at the end of each year for the next five years.

The rate of tax is 30% and tax is payable with a year's delay.

Electro can borrow from its bank at a rate of interest of 12.9% before tax.

What is the present value of the leasing costs?

Use a whole number for the cost of capital.

$ [   ]

3.15   HiFli Co has completed an investment appraisal and has made a decision to obtain a fleet of new aircraft. HiFli is now evaluating whether to *lease* the new aircraft or *buy* them using a bank loan to fully finance the acquisition.

Which of the following is the BEST discount rate to use for the LEASE *VERSUS* BUY evaluation?

O   A risk-adjusted weighted average cost of capital adjusted to reflect the change in gearing

O   The post-tax cost of HiFli's proposed loan

O   HiFli's cost of equity adjusted for the impact of the change in gearing

O   The pre-tax cost of HiFli's proposed loan

3.16   A company has decided to invest in a new asset and is now considering whether to lease the asset or buy it outright. The following calculations have been prepared to assist with the financing decision however they include some errors:

Buy option	T0	T1–4
	$	$
Purchase cost	(50,000)	
Tax relief on tax allowable depreciation		2,500
Interest on bank borrowings		(2,500)
Net cash flow	(50,000)	0
Discount factor @ 5%	1	3.546
Present value	(50,000)	0
NPV	(50,000)	

Lease option	T1–4
	$
Lease payment	(12,000)
Tax relief on lease payment	2,400
Net cash flow	(9,600)
Discount factor @ 5%	3.546
NPV	(34,042)

The following information is relevant:

- If the asset is purchased outright it will be financed by 5% bank borrowings.

- Life of the asset is four years.

- The asset has a zero residual value.

- The purchase price is eligible for tax-allowable depreciation on a straight-line basis.

- Corporate income tax rate is 20%, tax is payable in the year in which profits are earned.

- Lease details: four annual lease payments $12,000 to begin at the start of the lease on 1 January 20X1.

Which THREE of the following are valid criticisms of the above calculations prepared by the assistant accountant?

☐ Using a discount rate of 5% is incorrect.

☐ The tax allowable depreciation calculation in the buy option is incorrect.

☐ The timing of the tax relief on the lease payments is incorrect.

☐ It is incorrect to include the interest on the loan in the buy option.

☐ The timing of the lease payments are incorrect.

4 Equity finance

4.1 Trip Co is a new company that is making its first public issue of shares. It plans to do so by means of an offer for sale by tender.

The following tenders have been received:

Price tendered per share $	Millions of shares applied for at this price
3.00	50
2.90	100
2.80	250
2.70	500
2.60	1,000
2.50	1,700
2.40	2,400

The company has decided already that partial acceptance would mean allotting to each accepted applicant an equal proportion of the shares applied for.

If the company decides to issue exactly 3,000 million shares, how much money would be raised?

$ [   ] million

4.2 Freitag plc has a beta factor of 1.2 and a cost of equity of 9%. The risk-free rate of return is 3%.

What is the market rate of return?

[   ] %

4.3 A company has gearing of 50% (debt/debt + equity) and plans to:

- Issue $1.00 ordinary shares under a rights issue at a 40% discount to the current market price of $3.00 a share

- Reinvest the funds raised immediately in a project with an Internal Rate of Return (IRR) equal to WACC.

How is this plan likely to affect gearing and the share premium account?

Gearing (debt/debt + equity) [▼]

Share premium account [▼]

Picklist:

Stay the same
Decrease
Increase

4.4 The dividends and earnings of Bayle Eaves Co over the last five years have been as follows.

Year	Dividends	Earnings
	$	$
20X1	300,000	713,000
20X2	316,500	735,000
20X3	334,500	764,000
20X4	361,000	794,000
20X5	379,000	834,000

4 periods

The company is financed entirely by equity, and there have been 2,000,000 shares in issue over this period. The share price is currently $1.18 ex div.

On the assumption that the data for 20X1–20X5 provides a basis for estimating future trends, what is the cost of equity?

O 16%

O 21%

O 22%

O 23%

4.5 **What is unsystematic risk?**

O The risk that cannot be eliminated by diversification and is common to all firms

O The risk that can be eliminated by diversification

O The risk that remains when all the hedging techniques have been used by the firm

O The risk that the whole financial system will be affected by the failure of a key financial institution

---

4.6 Label each of the following statements as true or false:

	True	False
The capital asset pricing model can be used to calculate the cost of equity of an entity. Unlike the dividend growth model CAPM specifically factors risk into the calculation.	☐	☐
The beta factor is a measure of the total risk associated with a share or security.	☐	☐

4.7

Company B wishes to raise $3 million, using a 1 for 10 rights issue at $3.00, to invest in an environmental project that is estimated to deliver an NPV of $ 0.

If shareholders do not want to take part in the issue they can sell their rights to B for $0.20 per each share held.

B has 10 million shares in issue and B's share price on the day of the announcement of this project is $5.75.

B's theoretical ex-rights price is $5.50

Will shareholders who sell their rights to B be better off/worse off/no better or worse off than shareholders who take up their rights? ☐▼

Picklist:
Better off
Worse off
No better or worse off

4.8

Buckle Co has 500,000 ordinary shares of $1 in issue, which have a current market price of $3.50. The company makes a 1 for 4 rights issue at a price of $2.25. The rate of return on existing funds is 7% and the rate of return on the new funds is 9%.

What is the yield-adjusted theoretical ex-rights price?

$ ☐ to two decimal places.

4.9 50 million ordinary shares are to be offered to the general public by tender offer. Interested parties were invited to bid for shares in the range $2.20 to $2.60 per share. The results are as follows:

Price offered $	Number of share bids received at that price
2.20	5
2.30	35
2.40	55
2.50	44
2.60	25

Which of the following options shows how the shares will be allocated?

Select from column A, B, C or D.

Price Number of shares issued at each price (millions)

	A	B	C	D
$2.20	5	0	0	0
$2.30	35	0	0	0
$2.40	10	50	0	0
$2.50	0	0	50	25
$2.60	0	0	0	25

- ○ A
- ○ B
- ○ C
- ○ D

4.10 Sonntag Co has a weighted average cost of capital of 12%.

The market premium for risk is 6% and the risk-free rate of return is 3%.

Sonntag is an ungeared company.

What is Sonntag's asset beta?

Sonntag's beta factor is [   ] to one decimal place.

4.11 Company X will raise $150 million from a rights issue of shares, to finance a new project.

Which of the following are MOST likely to be affected by the choice of discount at which the shares are issued?

Select ALL that apply.

- ☐ Cost of underwriting
- ☐ WACC
- ☐ Earnings per share
- ☐ Shareholder wealth
- ☐ TERP

4.12 Which of the following correctly describes the calculation of the cost of equity using the capital asset pricing model (CAPM)?

- O Risk-free rate of return with an additional premium for unsystematic risk
- O Risk-free rate of return with a beta factor and the market rate of return added onto it
- O Risk-free rate of return plus the market rate of return
- O Risk-free rate of return with an additional premium for systematic risk

---

4.13 The following data has been taken from the annual reports of a single company:

Year ended 31 December	20X1	20X2	20X3	20X4
Earnings ($ million)	120	160	180	210
Number of shares in issue at the end of the year (million)	100	150	150	150

The company issued 50 million new shares by means of a rights issue on 3 January 20X2.

The latest annual report lists growth in earnings per share as a financial objective.

What is the compound average annual growth rate in earnings per share achieved between 20X1 and 20X4?

- O 5.3%
- O 5.6%
- O 20.5%
- O 25.0%

4.14 Which THREE of the following statements are correct?

- ☐ Standard deviation can be used to measure the systematic risk of a share.
- ☐ Systematic risk can only be reduced by investing in a diversified portfolio of investments.
- ☐ Unsystematic risk can only be reduced by investing in a diversified portfolio of investments.
- ☐ Investing in a share that has a high standard deviation can reduce systematic risk in the investor's portfolio.
- ☐ Unsystematic risk refers to the variability of returns from a share due to factors unique to the firm's context.
- ☐ Including one extra share in one's portfolio of investments will always reduce the unsystematic risk but not the systematic risk of the portfolio.

4.15 Company X is forecasting that its free cash flows to equity will be $150m and earnings will be $100m.

X is forecasting that earnings and dividends will grow by 3%, and that re-invested funds are predicted to earn a return of 10%.

Based on this forecast, what is the BEST prediction of the forecast dividend?

- O $70m
- O $30m
- O $45m
- O $105m

4.16   The shares of Crust Co are currently priced at $6.80. The company is about to announce a
        2 for 5 rights issue. The issue price of the new shares will be $5.75.

        What is the theoretical value of a right?

        O $0.15

        O $0.75

        O $0.30

        O $0.375

4.17   A company has:

        •   An equity beta of 0.8
        •   Pre-tax cost of debt of 4.2%
        •   Gearing (D/D+E) of 40%
        •   Corporate income tax rate of 20%

        The risk-free rate is 3% and an equity risk premium of 4%.

        The company's debt beta is: [▼]

        Picklist:

        0.09
        0.30
        0.32
        0.80
        1.20

4.18   Company Z has announced a 1 for 5 rights issue at a discount of 25% to the current share
        price of $2.80. The purpose of the rights issue is to finance a project with a yield of 16%.

        Company Z has a WACC of 12%, and has 500m $1 ordinary shares in issue.

        Corporate income tax is 25%.

        The yield-adjusted TERP is:

        $ [   ] to one decimal place.

5 Dividend policy

5.1 Almondvale have prepared a cash flow forecast as follows:

Amounts are in $s	April	May	June
Inflows	100,000	120,000	180,000
Outflows – expenses	(120,000)	(110,000)	(200,000)
Dividend – interim	(50,000)		
Capital expenditure		(120,000)	
Taxation	(90,000)		
Closing balance	(160,000)	(270,000)	(290,000)

The capital expenditure is a new machine that will gradually increase capacity but incurs a number of fixed costs. It has a positive NPV and is expected to generate positive monthly cash flows after two months. The interim dividend has not yet been declared but is widely anticipated. The company has an agreed overdraft of $250,000.

Which of the following actions would you recommend?

○ Cancel the interim dividend.

○ Defer the capital expenditure.

○ Defer the taxation payment.

○ Defer the interim dividend.

5.2 **In which of the following circumstances is a scrip dividend MOST likely to be preferable to a normal dividend?**

Select ALL that apply.

☐ For a bank wishing to increase its capital adequacy ratios

☐ To retain cash in a business to finance investment

☐ To finance a share buyback programme

☐ To reward shareholders after many years of not declaring a dividend

☐ To split the shares in order to make them more marketable

5.3 Angora Co has 100,000 ordinary shares in issue with a nominal value of $1 and a market value of $2.50.

It is proposing to make a 1 for 5 scrip bonus issue.

What will be the effect of the issue on the statement of financial position figures for issued share capital and reserves?

○ There will be no change to capital or reserves because no new finance is raised.

○ Issued share capital will increase by $20,000; reserves will be unchanged.

○ Issued share capital will increase by $20,000; reserves will decrease by $20,000.

○ Issued share capital will increase by $50,000; reserves will decrease by $20,000.

5.4   A company pursues a zero-dividend policy. It is funded largely by venture capital from an equity investor and the investor expects internally generated funds to be reinvested in the business.

This dividend policy is indicative of which of the following?

O   Clientèle effect

O   Signalling effect

O   Restrictive covenants

O   Multiplier effect

5.5   In recent years Company DEX has had the following financial results.

	20X3 $m	20X4 $m	20X5 $m
Profits attributable to ordinary shareholders	105.0	125.0	142.0
Dividend	33.6	40.0	45.4
Capital expenditure	89.0	116.0	29.6
Number of ordinary shareholders (millions)	280	280	280

DEX pays corporate income tax at 30%.

Which of the following BEST describes the dividend policy?

O   Residual

O   Progressive

O   Constant payout ratio

O   Irrelevant

5.6   Subtropic Ltd was incorporated one year ago. It has one single shareholder who is also the only director and employee. The company is entirely financed by equity and wishes to keep its gearing low. The objective of the company is to grow turnover and profits by 75% per average in each of the next three years.

Which of the following dividend policies would be MOST applicable to Subtropic Ltd?

O   Constant payout ratio

O   Stable growth

O   Residual

O   100% payout

5.7 The majority of Company TIJ's ordinary share capital is owned by institutional shareholders. These shareholders have a strong preference for high dividend payouts. This preference is mainly due to a tax exemption that the institutional shareholders receive in respect of dividend income.

In the current reporting period the board of Company TIJ has announced that they intend to maintain the dividend at the same level as in the previous period.

Which of the following factors is MOST likely to have been decisive when setting the dividend for the current reporting period in the scenario described?

- ○ Signalling effect
- ○ Clientèle effect
- ○ Gearing
- ○ Restrictive covenants

5.8 **Which of the following statements is consistent with Modigliani and Miller's dividend irrelevance theory?**

- ○ A policy of steady growth in dividend is preferable to a residual dividend policy.
- ○ Shareholder return can be measured as the aggregate of dividends plus growth in share price.
- ○ The share price is NOT affected by a dividend payment.
- ○ Shareholder wealth can be maximised by retaining a high percentage of earnings.

5.9 **In which of the following situations is a residual dividend policy MOST likely to be appropriate?**

- ○ A large publicly listed company
- ○ A small family-owned private company where the majority of the shareholders use dividend income to pay household expenses
- ○ A small company listed on a small company stock exchange and owned by investors seeking maximum capital growth on their investment
- ○ In a tax regime where individuals pay less tax on income than on capital gains

5.10 **Which THREE of the following statements are correct?**

- ☐ A share buyback will increase the level of liquidity of the company undertaking it
- ☐ A stock split will leave each shareholder with fewer shares
- ☐ A scrip dividend may lead to some shareholders receiving cash from the company
- ☐ An enhanced scrip dividend involves offering shareholders a choice between cash and shares
- ☐ A special dividend is the payment of cash to all the company's shareholders

5.11   Which of the following assumptions did Modigliani and Miller make when formulating their theory of dividend irrelevance?

Select ALL that apply.

☐   The cost of raising finance is a personal expense but not a corporate one.

☐   Buying and selling shares bore no administrative or transaction cost.

☐   Only companies paid taxes on their profits.

☐   Individuals paid capital gains tax only.

☐   Taxes did not exist.

5.12   Which of the following is not a valid reason why the directors of Company Z, a listed company, might decide to retain earnings rather than pay them out as dividends?

○   Finance from retained cash has no cost as a source of finance.

○   Z has historically paid out low dividends and Z's shareholders are known to be more interested in capital gains.

○   Retention of earnings avoids the possibility of a change in control resulting from an issue of new shares.

○   Retention of earnings allows the directors to undertake investment projects without involving the shareholders.

5.13   Which of the following is LEAST likely to be a benefit of a share repurchase scheme?

○   Finding a use for surplus cash

○   Increase in earnings per share

○   Increase in gearing to reduce the weighted average cost of capital

○   An immediate boost to shareholder wealth as they receive funds from the repurchase

5.14   Company Y is considering a plan to return surplus cash to shareholders by paying a special dividend, making it clear to investors that this is a one-off event. Company Y is concerned about the threat of a takeover. Currently Company Y has no unused bank facilities.

Which of the following is the MOST likely consequence of this plan?

○   The company would become more vulnerable to a hostile takeover bid.

○   Shareholder wealth would decrease by the value of the cash paid as a special dividend.

○   The company would become less able to respond promptly to new business opportunities.

○   The share price would rise due to the signalling effect of the special dividend.

5.15 Ace Co has set itself a target of increasing earnings and dividends by 13.5% per annum next year.

The investment needed to achieve this will be financed from retained earnings.
Ace's earnings in 20X0 were $720,000.

The management accountant has estimated that the average return on equity for Ace is 18%.

What level of dividends can the board declare in 20X0 while still meeting the financial target set for earnings?

$ [   ] in $'000

5.16 A listed company has 10 million $0.50 shares in issue. The company is planning to repurchase 2 million shares at $0.75.

The impact of this plan on the cash balance and earnings per share is:

	Before the share repurchase	After the share repurchase
Cash ($ million)	2.00	[▼]
Earning per share ($)	0.20	[▼]

Picklist:

0
0.2
0.25
0.5
1.5
2.0

5.17 A company has the following current capital structure:

	Book value in total	Market value of each security
Ordinary share capital ($0.50 shares)	$50 million	$1.50
Bonds ($100 nominal value)	$50 million	$110

The company has grown successfully and has cash reserves of $15 million. The directors have decided to return some wealth to the shareholders and intend to use the cash reserves to repurchase some of the company's shares at their current market value. They would like to assess the impact of the proposed share repurchase on the company's gearing ratio.

The company calculates gearing measured as debt/(debt + equity) using market values.

Assume there are no changes in the market value of each individual security.

What will be the company's gearing level after the share repurchase?

O   26.8%

O   47.8%

O   28.9%

O   58.8%

6 Capital structure

6.1 The cost of capital in Company A, an all-equity financed company, is 12%. Company B is identical except that it is 60% financed by equity and 40% financed by debt (at market values).

The cost of debt is 6% and the rate of tax is 25%.

According to Modigliani and Miller, what will be the weighted average cost of capital of Company B?

| | % to one decimal place.

6.2 Anders Ltd is a company based in a country called Scandovia. Its parent company is based in Roslakia. In Scandovia the corporate tax rate is 40% and in Roslakia it is 15%. In both countries a deduction from profits is available for interest payments and interest income is taxable.

A situation of thin capitalisation may arise in which of the following circumstances?

O   Parent company lends more to Anders Ltd than a commercial bank would

O   Parent company lends less to Anders Ltd than a commercial bank would

O   Parent company borrows a significant amount from Anders Ltd in order to repay its own debt

O   Anders Ltd has gearing that is lower than industry average

6.3 **For each set of circumstances state whether the company is likely to prefer to keep its financial gearing high or low:**

	High	Low
ABC Ltd was set up nine months ago and has ambitious growth targets over the next three years.	☐	☐
DEF Ltd operates in the high technology sector and has highly cyclical cash flows.	☐	☐
GHI Ltd operates in the service sector and has lots of intellectual capital but few tangible assets.	☐	☐

6.4 **According to the traditional theory of gearing which THREE of the following statements are incorrect?**

☐   The weighted average cost of capital of a company is determined purely by its gearing.

☐   The weighted average cost of capital of a company can be increased by decreasing gearing.

☐   The weighted average cost of capital can be minimised by using no debt.

☐   The weighted average cost of capital is optimised when it is at its lowest.

☐   The weighted average cost of capital is irrelevant to a company's value.

6.5 **Which THREE of the following would be valid reasons for significantly decreasing an entity's financial gearing?**

☐ The directors believe that the weighted average cost of capital would rise if gearing was reduced.

☐ The company has no taxable profits so cannot benefit from the tax shield.

☐ Loan covenants on existing debt specify that debt should be lower.

☐ Interest rates are expected to fall significantly over the next three years.

☐ Interest rates are expected to increase significantly over the next three years.

6.6 **The suggestion that the cost of equity of a company will increase as an ungeared company introduces debt into its capital structure for the first time but the weighted average cost of capital falls as a result of that increase in gearing comes from which of the following?**

Select ALL that apply.

☐ Modigliani and Miller's theory of gearing (without tax 1958)

☐ Modigliani and Miller's theory of gearing (with tax 1963)

☐ The traditional theory of gearing

☐ Arbitrage

☐ Trade-off theory

6.7 BT Co is purchasing a foreign company, WW, which will be set up as a subsidiary in Country Z. The currency of Country Z is the Z$.

Which of the following is MOST likely to influence BT to set up WW with a lower level of gearing?

○ High levels of political risk in Country Z

○ High levels of corporation tax in Country Z

○ A forecast fall in the value of the Z$

○ Thin capitalisation rules

6.8 **Label each of the following statements as true or false:**

	True	False
A rights issue is often preferred to a bank loan as a source of long-term funds because it prevents a reduction in earnings per share.	☐	☐
Operational gearing measures the degree to which a company uses debt to finance its operations	☐	☐
The ability to offer good quality security will usually reduce or maintain the interest rate offered by creditors	☐	☐

6.9   Company DK4 is an ungeared company and has a weighted average cost of capital of 14%. The company is about to introduce long-term debt into its capital structure in order to reduce its weighted average cost of capital.

This is consistent with which TWO theories?

☐   Interest rate parity theory

☐   Pecking-order theory

☐   Modigliani and Miller's theory with tax

☐   Modigliani and Miller's theory without tax

☐   The traditional theory of gearing

6.10   Company SV9 is an ungeared company with a cost of equity of 11% and is considering adjusting its gearing by taking out a loan at 5% and using it to buy back some equity. After the buyback Company SV9 will have a debt to equity ratio of 1:2. Corporation tax is 20%.

What will be the new cost of equity for Company SV9 according to Modigliani and Miller after the issue of new debt?

☐ _____ % one decimal place.

6.11   CER Co is about to issue long term debt for the first time to finance a project.

According to the traditional theory of gearing, what would happen to the weighted average cost of capital immediately after the issue?

○   Increase

○   Decrease

○   Unchanged

○   Need more information

6.12   A company plans to raise $30m of debt and to use these funds to repurchase shares.

Currently the company has a debt to equity ratio of 1 to 3 based on market values.

It currently has an ungeared cost of equity of 11% and a geared cost of equity of 13%, and a total market capitalisation of equity of $300m.

Corporate income tax is 30%.

According to Modigliani and Miller's theory with tax, the WACC after the buyback would become:

○ $12.61 = 13\left[1-\left[\dfrac{9}{300}\right]\right]$

○ $11.73 = 13\left[1-\left[\dfrac{39}{400}\right]\right]$

○ $9.41 = 11\left[1-\left[\dfrac{39}{270}\right]\right]$

○ $9.93 = 11\left[1-\left[\dfrac{39}{400}\right]\right]$

BPP
LEARNING
MEDIA

6.13 Company A is a leading tuition provider of accountancy training courses and is seeking to grow revenue by expanding the range of online courses it offers to students with the aim of growing the share price. If the expansion goes ahead expectations are that the share price will rise to $6.

To enable it to do this it needs to invest $50 million in new information technology systems. It is considering raising the finance through bank borrowings from its primary bank for a ten-year term at an interest rate of 5%.

Company A has a covenant on its existing loan as follows:

• Gearing levels as measured by long-term debt divided by long-term debt plus equity should not exceed 45% based on market values.

Company A is currently financed as follows:

Share capital   50 million ordinary shares with a nominal value of $1 each
Bank borrowings $150 million

If bank borrowings are used to fund the new investment which of the following statements are true?

☐   Gearing will be 67% and the bank covenant is breached.

☐   Gearing will be 40% and the bank covenant is not breached.

☐   Gearing will be 80% and the bank covenant is breached.

☐   Gearing will be 33% and the bank covenant is not breached.

6.14 Company A is an ungeared company. The following information is relevant:

• It has a cost of equity of 15%.
• It has 5 million $0.50 shares with a current market price of $5.
• The rate of corporate income tax is 20%.

The company is planning on taking out bank borrowings of $10 million and using all of the finance to repurchase some of its shares. Assume there is no change in Company A's share price.

What is Company A's expected weighted average cost of capital after the share repurchase?

| | % to one decimal place.

6.15 Company A and Company B are identical in all operating and risk characteristics but their capital structures differ. The following information is relevant:

Company A

Pre-tax cost of debt is 7%

Equity:Debt is 2:1

Company B

Only equity financed

Cost of equity is 15%

The rate of corporate income tax applicable to both companies is 20%

What is the cost of equity for Company A?

| | % to one decimal place.

7 Financial risk

7.1 **What is the purpose of hedging?**

O   To protect a profit already made from having undertaken a risky position

O   To make a profit by accepting risk

O   To reduce or eliminate exposure to risk

O   To reduce costs

7.2 Company A operates in Country A and owns 100% of the equity in a Company B who operates in Country B, where inflation rates are high. Company B buys all its raw materials from Company A and makes products for sale in neighbouring countries where the economy is stronger and inflation lower. Company B pays Company A using its own currency.

Which TWO of the following statements are correct?

☐   Company A is exposed to transaction risks. The currency received from Company B is likely to decline over time because of domestic inflationary pressures.

☐   Company A is exposed to translation risks. The currency received from Company B is likely to decline over time because of domestic inflationary pressures.

☐   Company B will be exposed to economic risk because it will almost certainly have to reflect the declining exchange rates in selling prices. This could make it difficult for Company B to make a profit.

☐   Company B could create a natural hedge by exporting products to the country where Company A is based in order to gain access to currency used by Company A.

7.3 **Which of the following is LEAST likely to be an advantage of using expatriate staff to run overseas operations compared with using local staff?**

O   Greater awareness of the organisation's culture and requirements

O   Possession of technical skills not available overseas

O   Lower costs

O   Easier control

7.4 A UK company expects to receive settlement of an export invoice worth USD 20 million. The current exchange rate between GBP and USD = US$2/£.

The daily volatility of this exchange rate = 0.5% and the standard normal value (Z) associated with a one-tail 99% confidence level is 2.33.

Calculate the one-day 99% value at risk (VaR).

£ [   ] to the nearest whole £.

7.5 What term is used to describe an organisation's exposures to the effect of currency changes on the values of assets and liabilities in its accounts?

○ Translation exposure

○ Structural exposure

○ Transaction exposure

○ Economic exposure

7.6 You work as a financial journalist for a well-known student publication and have been asked to create an informative article on the risks that affect cash flows for companies. You have sourced a number of articles which you think will help to explain a number of relevant risks and have created summaries of each one to show the editor of the student publication. The summaries include the following information:

Company S employs a number of people to manage purchases between itself and overseas suppliers – in this case, they use hedging contracts to manage the difference between year-end trade payables and the amount the actually company pays.

Company P has changed its supply base in the last six months to address a gradual decline in the competitiveness of its products, especially in the export market. This has required an outsourcing arrangement where components are assembled overseas where labour is cheaper and then imported to P's headquarters for their eventual despatch to customers.

Following a series of bad debts, Company Q has implemented a policy of screening customers by an innovative new online service that collects and analyses big data on individuals and companies and shares it for a subscription fee.

An interview with an expert valuer from Company R who has been able to create a database of exchange rates and apply it to properties across the world so the values of similar assets across the world can be benchmarked and risk assessed.

Match each of the following Company summaries with the relevant risk category that is being described in each case by selecting from the options below:

	Economic risk	Financial risk	Translation risk	Transaction risk
Company S	☐	☐	☐	☐
Company P	☐	☐	☐	☐
Company Q	☐	☐	☐	☐
Company R	☐	☐	☐	☐

7.7 A UK company trades with a company in Country A where the A$ is the functional currency.

The UK company expects to receive A$30 million.

The current exchange rate between the A$ and GBP is A$1.5/GBP

The daily volatility of the exchange rate is 0.5%

Calculate the one-day 95% value at risk (VaR).

£ _____

7.8 What term is used to describe an organisation's exposure to the effect of short-term currency changes on cash flow?

- O Translation risk
- O Political risk
- O Transaction risk
- O Economic risk

7.9 Company A operates in Country A and is just about to invest in Country B. It is considering raising local finance denominated in B$ to finance the investment.

Which THREE of the following statements about using local finance are correct?

- ☐ It can minimise interest rate risk
- ☐ It can minimise translation risk
- ☐ It can minimise transaction risk
- ☐ It can minimise political risk
- ☐ It can minimise value at risk

7.10 Company A, located in Country A, imports from Company B, located in Country B. Company A's long-term strategy is to sell its products worldwide. Company A is a single entity financed wholly by equity finance with its operations based solely in Country A. The government's in both Country A and Country B are stable.

Which of the following risks is/are Company A exposed to?

Select ALL that apply.

- ☐ Interest rate risk
- ☐ Political risk
- ☐ Economic risk
- ☐ Transaction risk
- ☐ Translation risk

8 Currency risk – exchange rates

8.1 Are the following statements correct or incorrect?

Statement 1 – A company is only exposed to currency risk if it exports or imports goods or services, or borrows or invests in a foreign currency.

Statement 2 – When interest rates on the euro are lower than interest rates on sterling a UK company with no other cash flows in euros will not save money by borrowing in euros.

- O Both statements are correct.
- O Both statements are incorrect.
- O Statement 2 only is correct.
- O Statement 1 only is correct.

8.2 Lytham plc trade in Southeast Asia and remit profits to the UK. They are considering methods that they can use to minimise their exposure to foreign exchange risk.

Which of the following will NOT protect them from exchange risks?

○ Matching

○ Forward contracts

○ Leading and lagging

○ Invoicing in the overseas currency

8.3 The current spot rate for the US dollar against sterling is £1 = $2.45.

If the US experiences inflation at 2% each year over the next two years, and if the UK experiences inflation at 5% each year over the same period, what movements in the exchange rate should we expect in that time?

○ Sterling will depreciate by about 3%.

○ Sterling will depreciate by about 6%.

○ Sterling will appreciate by about 6%.

○ Sterling will appreciate by about 3%.

8.4 A British company is due to receive an amount of €10,000,000 from a French customer. The current spot rate quoted is £1 = €1.2525 – 1.2550.

To the nearest £, how much will the UK company receive?

○ £7,968,127

○ £7,984,032

○ £12,550,000

○ £12,525,000

8.5 The US dollar/sterling spot rate is £1 = $1.52.

One-year US interest rates = 8%

One-year UK interest rates = 14%

The one-year forward exchange rate between the dollar and sterling should be:

○ $1.4400 to £1

○ $1.6112 to £1

○ $1.4288 to £1

○ $1.6044 to £1

8.6 Using the following data, what £/$ exchange rate to four decimal places would be predicted for a year in the future using interest rate parity?

The current spot rate is £1 = $1.6500.

Current interest rates are 2.0% in the UK and 3.5% in the USA.

£1 = $

[   ] to four decimal places.

8.7 Chocshop distributes exotic chocolates from around the world. It buys chocolates from Ruritania which cost Ruritanian $130,000 and the goods are resold in the UK for £42,500. At the time of importation, the exchange rate is £1 = R$ 3.4050 – 3.6000.

What is the expected profit or loss on the resale of the chocolates in the UK?

O £4,321 profit

O £6,898 loss

O £6,389 profit

O £5,384 loss

8.8 Consider the following statements concerning currency risk:

1. Leading and lagging is a method of hedging transaction exposure.
2. Matching receipts and payments is a method of hedging translation exposure.

Which of the above statements is/are true?

O Statement 1 true; Statement 2 true

O Statement 1 false; Statement 2 false

O Statement 1 true; Statement 2 false

O Statement 1 false; Statement 2 true

8.9 A UK company is about to enter two transactions receiving an amount of €9,112,500 from a Dutch company and paying an amount of $7,600,000 to an American company.

Current exchange rates are: €1 = £0.8 and £1 = $1.9.

What will the company receive and pay in £?

O Receives £11,390,625; Pays £4,000,000

O Receives £7,290,000; Pays £4,000,000

O Receives £7,290,000; Pays £14,440,000

O Receives £11,390,625; Pays £14,440,000

8.10   A group of companies controlled from the USA has subsidiaries in the UK, South Africa and Denmark. Below, these subsidiaries are referred to as UK, SA and DE respectively. At 31 March 20X8, inter-company indebtedness is as follows:

Debtor	Creditor	Amount
UK	SA	3,500,000 South African rand (R)
UK	DE	1,400,000 Danish kroner (Kr)
DE	SA	2,300,000 South African rand
SA	UK	£240,000 sterling
SA	DE	1,150,000 Danish kroner

It is the company's policy to net off inter-company balances to the greatest extent possible. The central treasury department is to use the following exchange rates for this purpose.

US$1 equals R6 / £0.70 / Kr 5.8.

Which of the following would be a possible arrangement for settling inter-subsidiary indebtedness?

O   The UK subsidiary pays $56,322 to the Danish subsidiary and receives $425,533 from the South African subsidiary.

O   The UK subsidiary pays $425,533 to the South African subsidiary and pays $56,322 to the Danish subsidiary.

O   The UK subsidiary receives $56,322 from the Danish subsidiary and pays $425,533 to the South African subsidiary.

O   The UK subsidiary receives $425,533 from the South African subsidiary and receives $56,322 from the Danish subsidiary.

9   Managing currency risk

9.1   Lanvert SA is a French company which trades frequently with the USA.

It has a net payment of $2.8 million to make in three months' time.

The following information is relvant:

Exchange rates	€ per $1
Spot	1.0610–1.0661
Three-months' forward	1.0650–1.0715
Six-months' forward	1.0683–1.0740

What is the amount that can be guaranteed to be paid in three months' time using a forward contract?

€ [   ] million (give your answer to the nearest whole million €.)

9.2 **What is the maximum liability of the writer of a call option?**

○   Exercise price + Premium

○   Unlimited

○   Exercise price – Premium

○   Zero

9.3 A US company has made a sale to a customer in France for €1 million, with payment due in two months.

How could the company hedge its exchange rate exposure during this period using currency futures or options on currency futures?

○   Buy euro futures or buy put options on euro futures.

○   Buy euro futures or buy call options on euro futures.

○   Sell euro futures or buy call options on euro futures.

○   Sell euro futures or buy put options on euro futures.

9.4 Typha plc, a UK business, has recently sold goods to a US customer and expects to be paid $300,000 in three months' time. Typha plc enters into a forward exchange contract to sell $300,000 in three months' time to protect against foreign exchange risk. Exchange rates are:

$ spot	1.4505–1.4545
Three-months' forward	$0.0025–0.0020 pm

What is the sterling amount that will be received by the company in three months' time using a forward contract?

○   £205,973

○   £206,540

○   £207,182

○   £206,612

BPP
LEARNING
MEDIA

9.5 Lanvert SA is a French company which trades frequently with the USA. It has a net payment in three months time of $2.8 million to make.

Euro market traded option prices (62,500 euro contract size) in the USA. (The options relate to the purchase or sale of euros.)

Exercise price ($/€1)	June contracts		September contract	
	Calls	Puts	Calls	Puts
0.936	1.65	0.41	2.38	0.71
0.938	0.56	1.20	1.01	1.57
0.940	0.17	2.65	0.48	3.45

Option premia are in cents per euro and are payable up front. The options are American style. Assume that it is now 1 June and that option contracts mature on the 15th of the month.

How many options contracts should Lanvert enter into to hedge the full amount of the transaction given, assuming a rate of $0.938/euro?

- ○ 50
- ○ 46
- ○ 52
- ○ 48

9.6 The sterling/US dollar spot rate is £1 = $1.7770–1.7860 and the forward rate is quoted as 0.35–0.36 discount.

At what forward rate will the bank sell US dollars?

- ○ 1.7724
- ○ 1.7896
- ○ 1.7735
- ○ 1.7805

9.7 The current spot rate for US dollar/South African rand is $1 = R6.7580–6.7600. The three-month forward rate is quoted as 0.0100–0.0090 premium. You wish to convert R2 million into US dollars in three months' time, and you intend to hedge the currency exposure with a forward exchange contract.

How many US dollars will you receive in three months' time?

- ○ $296,384
- ○ $295,464
- ○ $295,508
- ○ $296,252

9.8   Easter Inc, an American company, buys some of its goods from Australia. The most recent invoice is for A$1,300,000 which is due in two months' time. The current exchange rate is A$2.80. It has been offered a forward contract to buy Australian dollars at A$2.90 in two months' time. The exchange rate is not expected to go above A$3.00.

What is the maximum risk that Easter would be exposed to if the company decided to hedge this expense using the forward contract?

Maximum exposure is $\boxed{\text{\$ \hspace{3cm}}}$ to the nearest $.

9.9   PLW Inc has entered a transaction that will involve a yen payment exposure arising in six months' time. The company's treasurer decides to cover the exposure by means of foreign currency options, and buys a six-month yen call/dollar put option.

Forward exchange rate   240 yen = $1
Option strike price   240 yen = $1
Option premium   1.2%

What is the worst case effective exchange rate that the company will have to pay, and what would it do in six months' time if the spot rate is 245 yen = $1?

O   237.1   Exercise the option.

O   242.9   Let option lapse.

O   237.1   Let option lapse.

O   242.9   Exercise the option.

9.10   Edted, a company based in the Eurozone, hedged a payment of DKr5,550,000 it was due to make in six months' time to a Danish supplier by buying an over-the-counter call option at €1 = DKr7.4.

Edted is now due to make the payment and the current exchange rate is €1 = DKr7.5.

What will be the cost in € to Edted?

€ $\boxed{\hspace{3cm}}$

9.11   An engineering company has entered into a futures contract requiring it to deliver an agreed amount of KRW (South Korean Won) to a counterparty in three months' time.

Which of the following BEST describes the likely impact on the engineering company's margin if the value of the KRW rises against the company's home currency?

O   Some of the margin paid to date will be returned to the company.

O   The margin will remain unchanged.

O   Additional funds will need to be deposited by the engineering company.

O   The margin will have to be renegotiated between the two parties to this contract.

BPP
LEARNING
MEDIA

9.12   CJI is a UK company importing goods from a US supplier on 60 days credit. It is concerned about the exchange rate depreciating. It can obtain Sterling futures contracts of £62,500 each which are currently trading on the futures market at a rate of US$1.4400 per £. It has decided to enter into an arrangement to use 10 of these futures contracts but needs advice on how to set them up properly.

One of the non-executive board members of CJI is keen to understand more about the process of using currency futures. He has done some research and compiled a 'quick guide' which explains some of the terminology used. He has asked you to review this for accuracy as he is concerned he may have used some terms incorrectly.

Match each of the following terms with the description from the picklist of definitions below:

Closing out a contract   [▼]

Basis risk   [▼]

Margin requirements   [▼]

Picklist:

The underlying volatility that exists between the futures price and the spot rate of exchange used for hedging

The minimum amount of profit required by the company to justify the hedge being used

The underlying volatility of the spot exchange rate used for hedging

The controls used when completing a futures transaction

The process used when completing a futures transaction

The minimum amount of money required by the exchange before a futures contract can be agreed

---

9.13   CJI is a UK company importing goods from a US supplier on 60 days credit. It is concerned about the exchange rate depreciating. It can obtain Sterling futures contracts of £62,500 each which are currently trading on the futures market at a rate of US$1.4400 per £. It has decided to enter into an arrangement to use 10 of these futures contracts but needs advice on how to set them up properly.

It is 60 days later and CJI now needs to pay its supplier. The exchange rate has moved against CJI: consequently, it will need to pay more for its supplies on the spot market than at the time of importing the goods. As part of the process of closing out the futures contracts for CJI you have been asked to calculate the outcome on the futures market.

Assuming there has been a movement of 100 ticks on each contract, what will be the total outcome of the futures contracts?

O   A loss of £6,250

O   A loss of US$6,250

O   A gain of US$6,250

O   A gain of £6,250

9.14 A US company wishes to hedge the future receipt of £1,000,000 from a customer in the UK and is concerned the spot rate of exchange will depreciate and they will receive fewer US$ than the current exchange rate would deliver. They have decided to use over-the-counter (OTC) sterling currency options and need to arrange them with their bank via a broker.

What arrangement will the broker discuss with the bank?

○ US$ call options

○ £ call options

○ £ put options

○ US$ put options

9.15 Company C is based in Country C, where the currency is the C$. Company C is expecting the following transactions with suppliers and customers who are based in Europe.

One month: Expected receipt of 240,000 euros
One month: Expected payment of 140,000 euros
Three months: Expected receipts of 300,000 euros

A one-month forward rate of 1.7832 euros per $1 has been offered by the company's bank and the spot rate is 1.7822 euros per $1.

Other relevant financial information is as follows:

Three-month European borrowing rate   1.35%
Three-month Country C deposit rate   1.15%

What are the expected dollar receipts in three months using a money market hedge?

○ $167,999

○ $296,004

○ $166,089

○ $164,201

9.16 A US company owes a European company €3.5m due to be paid in 3 months' time. The spot exchange rate is $1.96–$2:€1 currently. Annual interest rates in the two locations are as follows:

	Borrowing	Deposit
US	8%	3%
Europe	5%	1%

What will be the equivalent US$ value of the payment using a money market hedge?

○ $6,965,432

○ $6,979,750

○ $7,485,149

○ $7,122,195

---

10 Managing interest rate risk

10.1 Which of the following is the BEST description of interest rate risk?

- ○ The risk from borrowing funds.
- ○ The risk from not being able to meet interest payments on borrowings.
- ○ The risk to profits, cash-flows or even a company's valuation from any change in interest rates.
- ○ The risk that interest rates will rise.

10.2 A company wishes to arrange a collar to fix a future interest rate on a variable rate five-year loan it has obtained from Gross Bank.

By arranging the collar, the company will effectively be:

- ○ Selling a cap and buying a floor
- ○ Buying a cap and buying a floor
- ○ Selling a cap and selling a floor
- ○ Buying a cap and selling a floor

10.3 Which of the following are disadvantages of using interest rate futures?

Select ALL that apply.

- ☐ Contracts are subject to basis risk.
- ☐ Contracts are limited to a set amount of borrowing by fixed contract values.
- ☐ Contracts are closed out on a specified date.
- ☐ Contracts are only available for borrowing in a limited number of currencies.

10.4 A company has a floating rate loan of £4 million with four years remaining to maturity, on which it pays interest of LIBOR plus 50 basis points, but it would prefer to pay a fixed rate of interest on this loan amount. It therefore arranges a 'plain vanilla' four-year interest rate swap. The bank's rates for a four-year swap are 5.50%–5.55%.

What is the effective net interest rate that the company will pay, as a result of arranging the swap?

- ○ 5.05%
- ○ 5.0%
- ○ 6.0%
- ○ 6.05%

10.5 In three months' time you will have £6 million to put on deposit for four months. You are concerned that interest rates will fall and wish to arrange an FRA to hedge the risk and fix an effective interest rate for the future deposit.

What will you do to hedge the exposure?

- ○ Sell a 3 v 7 FRA
- ○ Buy a 3 v 4 FRA
- ○ Sell a 3 v 4 FRA
- ○ Buy a 3 v 7 FRA

10.6 Three-month sterling June futures are quoted on LIFFE at 93.50. Call options on three-month sterling June futures at 93.00 are quoted at 0.66.

This premium of 0.66 represents:

- ○ 0.66 intrinsic value
- ○ 0.66 time value
- ○ 0.50 intrinsic value and 0.16 time value
- ○ 0.16 intrinsic value and 0.50 time value

10.7 **Which of the following statements is correct?**

- ○ If interest rates rise, the market price of interest rate futures will fall.
- ○ If interest rates rise, the market price of interest rate futures will rise.
- ○ If interest rates rise, the coupon rate on a bond will fall.
- ○ If interest rates rise, the coupon rate on a bond will rise.

10.8 **Which of the following instruments is MOST similar to a forward rate agreement (FRA)?**

- ○ An interest rate guarantee (IRG)
- ○ An interest rate swap
- ○ An interest rate option
- ○ An interest rate future

10.9 The spot rate of exchange is £1 = $1.4400. Annual interest rates are 4% in the UK and 10% in the USA. Assume three months to be exactly one quarter of a year.

The three-month forward rate of exchange should be?

- ○ £1 = $1.5264
- ○ £1 = $1.4614
- ○ £1 = $1.4616
- ○ £1 = $1.5231

10.10   W Ltd has a six-month revolving loan facility for £2 million with its bank. This is reset every six months, agreed three months in advance of it taking effect. The finance director of W believes that interest rates will rise in the next six months and has decided to use a forward rate agreement (FRA) to hedge this borrowing.

Current base rates are 6% and W can access a 3–9 FRA at 6.1%.

Calculate the amount of interest paid for the next reset period if interest rates rise to 7%.

£ [   ] to the nearest £.

10.11   Lucas Lodge Hotels plc wishes to borrow £20 million for four years at a fixed rate of interest and Hunsford plc wishes to borrow £20 million for four years at a floating rate of interest. Each company can borrow the required amount as follows:

	Floating rate	Fixed rate
		%
Lucas Lodge Hotels plc	LIBOR plus 60 basis points	6.8
Hunsford plc	LIBOR plus 120 basis points	7.0

Assuming the companies agree to an interest rate swap and any benefits are shared equally, what will be the annual net interest cost for Lucas Lodge Hotels plc?

O   6.6%

O   6.4%

O   6.7%

O   6.5%

10.12   The treasurer of BU Ltd needs to borrow cash (in sterling or GBP) in November and is worried that interest rates will rise soon after.

Which of the following would be an appropriate hedging transaction for the treasurer to use?

O   Sell December short sterling futures.

O   Buy September short sterling futures.

O   Buy December short sterling futures.

O   Sell September short sterling futures.

10.13   A company has arranged a three-year variable rate loan at LIBOR plus 50 basis points. It
         has also arranged an interest rate collar that fixes a maximum effective borrowing cost for
         the company of 8.50% and a minimum effective borrowing cost of 7.50%.

         What does the collar consist of?

         O   With the collar, the company has bought a series of consecutive interest rate put
              options at a strike price of 8% and bought a matching series of call options at 8%.

         O   With the collar, the company has bought a series of consecutive interest rate put
              options at a strike price of 8% and sold a matching series of call options at 7%.

         O   With the collar, the company has bought a series of consecutive interest rate put
              options at a strike price of 8% and bought a matching series of call options at 7%.

         O   With the collar, the company has bought a series of consecutive interest rate put
              options at a strike price of 8% and sold a matching series of call options at 8%.

10.14   Company X manufactures domestic hot drinks machines and is investing in a new range of
         disposable containers for each drink supplied. This is going to require additional working
         capital of $12 million which will need to be available in three months' time. The financial
         controller of X has estimated that this will only be required to 'kick-start' the production
         process and that after a six-month period, there will be sufficient improvement in the
         company's liquidity from supplying these new containers to allow the funding to be repaid.

         Following discussions with the treasury function at X, the financial controller has decided to
         fund this using additional borrowing. However, given her concerns that the current LIBOR
         rate of 4.5% may soon rise and affect the margins earned from this new investment, she
         has decided to seek assistance from X's bank by using a forward rate agreement (FRA) to
         supplement the company's existing borrowing rate of LIBOR + 0.3%.

         The bank has quoted the following FRA rates: 3–9 for 4.7–4.6%.

         Assume the LIBOR rate in three months' time has risen to 5.1%.

         Which of the following statements are correct?

         Select ALL that apply.

         ☐   The effective rate paid by Company X will be 5.0%.

         ☐   The effective rate paid by Company X will be 4.9%.

         ☐   The effective rate paid by Company X will be 4.7%.

         ☐   The effective rate paid by Company X will be 4.6%.

         ☐   The FRA will result in a saving of 0.4%.

         ☐   The FRA will result in a saving of 0.5%.

10.15   **Which of the following objectives can be fulfilled by the use of cross-currency swaps?**

         Select ALL that apply.

         ☐   Reduction of currency risk

         ☐   Reduction of borrowing costs

         ☐   Reduction in risk of default

         ☐   Reduction in gearing

10.16   A company wants to borrow $5 million at a fixed rate of interest for three years, but can only raise the finance by borrowing from a bank at LIBOR plus 50 basis points. A bank arranges a three-year plain vanilla swap at a rate of 5.65%. The LIBOR reference rate is fixed at 6.0%.

What will be the payment under the swap for the period?

○   The company will pay the bank 0.15%.

○   The company will pay the bank 0.35%.

○   The company will pay the bank 0.85%.

○   The bank will pay the company 0.35%.

10.17   **Which of the following are valid reasons for a company preferring to borrow at a variable rate instead of a fixed rate?**

Select ALL that apply.

☐   In the short term the interest rate is likely to be lower

☐   Interest rates are expected to rise

☐   To alter the balance of the debt portfolio so that interest rate risk will be lower

☐   Variable rate loans are easier to renegotiate

☐   To increase the certainty of cash flow planning

10.18   **Label each of the following statements as true or false.**

	True	False
A currency swap can be used to manage currency risk and reduce borrowing costs.	☐	☐
A currency swap usually involves the swap of interest payment obligations between the counterparties but not the capital sums borrowed.	☐	☐
A currency swap can reduce the borrowing costs of all counterparties as long as they wish to borrow in the currency in which they have a comparative advantage.	☐	☐

10.19   Company S can borrow $42 million at a variable rate of LIBOR + 3%. Company T can borrow $42 million at a variable rate of LIBOR + 3.5%.

Company S can borrow the same amount at a fixed rate of 6.5% and Company T can borrow at a fixed rate of 6.8%

What is the potential saving before bank fees to be shared between Company S and Company T?

○   Nil

○   0.1%

○   0.2%

○   0.3%

10.20   Company A can raise debt in the variable rate market at LIBOR + 2% or 4% in the fixed rate market.

Company B can raise debt in the variable rate market at LIBOR + 2.3% or 4.1% in the fixed rate market.

Which of the following statements are true?

Select ALL that apply.

☐   Company A has absolute advantage in the debt market.

☐   Company A has comparative advantage in the variable rate market.

☐   Company A has comparative advantage in the fixed rate market.

☐   A swap may be arranged to benefit both companies.

☐   Only Company B can benefit from a swap in these circumstances.

11   Context of business valuations

11.1   Company A is a food manufacturer located in Country A. It is planning to acquire Company B, a food manufacturer in Country B.

Which THREE of the following are MOST likely to be considered a sales synergy in the event of the acquisition?

☐   Larger entity being able to borrow at lower interest rates

☐   Greater presence at marketing events

☐   Efficient use of tax losses within the new group

☐   Creation of a more streamlined hierarchy

☐   Increased shelf space in supermarkets devoted to the merged entity's products due to better bargaining power

☐   Access to new markets

11.2   **Which THREE of the following BEST describes the main aims of most competition authorities?**

☐   To ensure healthy levels of competition and safeguarding the public interest

☐   To prevent large mergers that create a firm with a market share of over 25%

☐   To promote fair and ethical competitive behaviour

☐   To ensure that governments do not restrict overseas competition by the use of trade barriers

☐   To investigate all mergers and takeovers

11.3   A company that operates several luxury restaurants which cater for affluent customers is about to launch a takeover bid for a company which runs a chain of fast food restaurants.

This is an example of which type of acquisition?

○   Horizontal

○   Backward vertical

○   Forward vertical

○   Conglomerate

11.4 Match the following disadvantages for a food retailer with the types of acquisition MOST likely to generate them.

Use each option only once.

	Horizontal	Vertical	Conglomerate
Being forced by the competition authorities to close down some of the stores owned by the acquired company	☐	☐	☐
Damage to the brand name because of lack of appropriate competences in the industry of the newly acquired company	☐	☐	☐
Being tied into using the in-house supplies provided by the newly acquired subsidiary	☐	☐	☐

11.5 A company based in Country A plans to launch a takeover bid for a company based in Country B. Country A has higher tax rates than Country B. Once the acquisition is complete company A plans to sell goods and services to Company B.

The group would wish to maximise post-tax profits but the government in Country A is considering the introduction of anti-tax avoidance legislation to prevent companies obtaining an artificial tax advantage from their transfer pricing policies.

Which TWO of the following statements are correct?

☐ Post-tax profits would be maximised if a high transfer price was charged for the goods and services mentioned

☐ Post-tax profits would be maximised if a low transfer price was charged for the goods and services mentioned

☐ Anti-tax avoidance legislation in Country A is likely to impose a minimum transfer price

☐ Anti-tax avoidance legislation in Country A is likely to impose a maximum transfer price

11.6 Match the following scenarios with the types of acquisition.

	Conglomerate	Horizontal	Backward vertical	Forward vertical
A firm of estate agents acquiring a local construction company	☐	☐	☐	☐
An undertaker acquiring another undertaker in a different part of the same country	☐	☐	☐	☐
A supermarket acquiring a farm	☐	☐	☐	☐

11.7 The Jordasian government has recently introduced legislation in its own country which allows overseas companies to use brought forward losses in Jordasian companies to reduce the tax liability of overseas parent companies.

All other things being equal, which of the following statements is correct?

   O   This tax law will increase the attractiveness of Jordasian companies as takeover targets.

   O   This tax law will reduce the incidence of cross-border acquisitions involving Jordasian companies.

   O   This tax law will make it more difficult for international groups that include Jordasian companies to trade in goods and services.

   O   This tax law will make it easier for Jordasian companies to launch successful takeover bids of overseas companies.

11.8 **Match the following terms to their definitions.**

	Economies of scale	Synergies	Golden parachutes	Poison pills
The additional value generated from combining together two companies over and above that which would be generated if the companies were kept separate	☐	☐	☐	☐
Large severance pay deals for directors triggered by a serious takeover bid by a third party	☐	☐	☐	☐
Savings in cost that are generated by an entity becoming larger	☐	☐	☐	☐

11.9 Company RS agreed to purchase Company T at a cash price of $120 million and estimates that there will be synergistic benefits of $25 million arising from the purchase.

Company T is wholly equity financed and has a market capitalisation of $110 million.

How much do Company RS's shareholders expect to gain from the deal?

   O $20 million

   O $15 million

   O $10 million

   O $5 million

11.10 **Which THREE of the following are more likely to be advantages of horizontal acquisition rather than conglomerate acquisition?**

   ☐   Economies of scale

   ☐   Reduction of competition

   ☐   Reducing risk by creating a broader portfolio

   ☐   Acquisition of undervalued companies

   ☐   Securing key elements of the value chain

   ☐   Increased market power

11.11 Which of the following types of acquisition is MOST likely to lead to the intervention by competition authorities?

- ○ One where post-acquisition integration problems are likely
- ○ Horizontal
- ○ Conglomerate
- ○ Cross-border

11.12 The directors of Company A, which owns and operates a national network of petrol stations, are exploring the acquisition of a petroleum distribution company, B.

B has had some critical exposure in the press because of its treatment of its staff. B is also the sole supplier to many of A's competitors.

B has been struggling in recent years so it is expected that a low price would be accepted for the acquisition of their business

Which of the following stakeholders are likely to be MOST concerned by this potential acquisition?

Select ALL that apply.

- ☐ A's competitors
- ☐ A's shareholders
- ☐ The competition authorities
- ☐ A's customers

11.13 S is a venture capital firm which provides significant funds to businesses engaged in the development of new technology in the medical sector. S is negotiating an equity finance package for a start-up business, D. Firm S wishes to invest in D for a maximum of four years, after which S wishes to withdraw from its investment.

Which THREE of the following are likely to provide a satisfactory exit route for S?

- ☐ Grant an option to D to borrow funds from S in four years so it can buy its shares back from S
- ☐ Plan to float the D shares on a stock exchange in four years
- ☐ An equity ratchet in the event of poor returns
- ☐ Sell the D shares in four years time to a private equity firm for cash
- ☐ Arrange for the D directors to buy back the shares from S in the third and fourth years of the investment for cash

11.14 Which of the following BEST defines vertical acquisitions?

- ○ The acquisition of one company by another where the two companies are in a similar but not identical line of business
- ○ The acquisition of one company by another where the two companies achieve significant cost synergies
- ○ The acquisition of one company by another where the companies operate in different lines of business
- ○ The acquisition of one company by another where previously one company was a customer of another

11.15   Which TWO of the following are MOST likely to be considered a management synergy in the event of a horizontal acquisition?

☐   Allocation of a greater pool of managers to projects in order to optimise the use of their skills

☐   Sharing best practice with regard to technology

☐   Sharing networks of distributors and retailers

☐   More efficient use of tax losses

☐   Spreading risk over a broader range of products

11.16   Company A is a car manufacturer, it operates in many countries but its domestic market is in Country A.

Company A is in the process of acquiring Company B, another company that is based in Country A. Company B specialises in (only) electric cars, which Company A does not currently produce.

Following the acquisition, Company A would grow in size by 20% in volume terms.

Which THREE of the following would be MOST likely to be synergistic benefits to Company A of purchasing Company B?

☐   Cost savings due to economies of scale in purchasing

☐   Reduction in staff costs due to elimination of duplicated administration roles

☐   A reduction in the volatility of cash flows due the diversification of its activities

☐   Cash benefit by sale and leaseback of the acquired factories

☐   Enhanced profit due to reduced competition in Country A

11.17   A food manufacturer based in USA acquires a food retailer in the UK.

This is an example of which type of acquisition?

O   Horizontal
O   Backward vertical
O   Forward vertical
O   Conglomerate

11.18   Lux Air is a large family owned regional business that produces individually designed luxury aircraft interiors has a number of investment opportunities and is considering the use of venture capital finance.

Which of the following investment opportunities is MOST likely to be appropriate for attracting venture capital finance?

O   A programme of planned replacement of existing manufacturing equipment entailing an investment of $10,000 per year over the next three years

O   Acquisition of major new building, which will replace the existing premises which is leased; this will provide slightly larger manufacturing capacity

O   A 10% expansion of the design consultancy division, which represents 10% of Lux Air's sales

O   An acquisition of Office Direct Co, a firm that operates in the same region supplying luxury office refurbishments

11.19 Company A, has launched a takeover bid of a competitor company operating in the same industry, Company B.

Company A has a large surplus cash balance and sees the acquisition as an opportunity to enhance shareholder wealth through the realisation of synergistic benefits.

Which THREE of the following would be MOST likely to be synergistic benefits to A of purchasing B?

☐ Cost savings in production due to economies of scale

☐ Cost savings in purchasing due to vertical integration

☐ Enhanced profit due to reduced competition

☐ Reduction in financial risk due to diversification

☐ Reduction in staff costs due to the removal of duplicated roles

11.20 Company K is a listed car manufacturer company. It is looking to acquire Company W, a small unlisted company specialising in manufacturing self drive cars.

Company K is considering financing the bid by either a cash offer financed by raising additional debt finance or a share issue.

Which of the following is an advantage to Company K of financing the bid with a share issue compared to a cash bid financed by debt?

○ Avoiding dilution of control

○ Earnings per share will increase

○ Gearing will decrease

○ Dividend per share will increase

12 Introduction to valuation methods

12.1 Share prices quoted on a stock exchange are observed to reflect historical share price information and other historical information about a company, but also respond to other information about the company immediately it becomes publicly available.

Which of the following BEST describes this form of market efficiency?

○ Weak form

○ Strong form

○ Semi-strong form

○ Semi-weak form

12.2

	Earnings for the year $ million	P/E ratio
Company 1	200	6
Company 2	320	5
Company 3	400	3.5

Rank the companies in order of market value by choosing from the picklist below.

(First being the highest and third being the lowest)

Highest value: [▼]

[▼]

Lowest value: [▼]

Picklist:

Company 1
Company 2
Company 3

12.3   KP Co is an ungeared company that has grown rapidly in recent years, it has a market capitalisation of $800 million and has 16 million shares in issue. KP's profits after tax are $40 million.

KP is considering an investment that would cost $100 million, and would earn additional cash inflows with a projected present value of $140 million.

KP proposes to fund this with cash generated from internal activities in order to preserve its ungeared capital structure.

How much will KP's share price increase by if the project is undertaken?

[   ] cents (give your answer to the nearest cent).

12.4   Company X has $200 million (nominal value) of $0.50 shares (nominal value) in issue with a market capitalisation of $400 million cum div. A dividend of $0.10/share has just been declared.

What is the total market capitalisation of Company X on an ex-div basis?

$ [   ] to the nearest million.

BPP
LEARNING
MEDIA

12.5 The statement of financial position of Naught Ltd is as follows.

	$	$
Non-current assets (net book value)		1,600,000
Inventory	1,048,000	
Receivables (less provision of 1% for doubtful debts)	792,000	
		1,840,000
Trade payables	1,080,000	
		(1,080,000)
		2,360,000
Share capital and reserves		2,360,000

The estimated realisable values of Naught Ltd's assets are as follows:

	$
Non-current assets	1,200,000
Inventory	1,160,000

It is generally agreed that 2% of total debtors will be uncollectable.

What would be the asset-based valuation of Naught Ltd using net realisable value?

- ○ $2.10m
- ○ $2.06m
- ○ $2.36m
- ○ $3.18m

12.6 AC Co has 200 million shares in issue. AC's latest reported profits after tax are $120 million and its shares have a market price of $6.

AC is planning an investment costing $200 million, which would be financed by a rights issue of 1 for 4 at a 33.3% discount.

After the rights issue AC's P/E ratio is expected to rise by 20% to reflect AC's increased growth potential. Earnings are expected to stay constant.

Assuming that this estimate is accurate, what will be the outcome of this?

- ○ A $0.24 drop in the share price and a $40m increase in total shareholder wealth
- ○ A $0.24 drop in the share price and a $60m decrease in total shareholder wealth
- ○ A $1.20 rise in the share price and a $400 million increase in total shareholder wealth
- ○ A $0.24 drop in the share price and a $240m increase in total shareholder wealth

---

12.7 XR Co estimates that it will pay no dividends for the next three years. After this it plans to pay a dividend of $0.40 / share, which will then grow at 5% per year.

XR's shareholders expected return is 15%.

What is the estimated value of a share in XR Co?

[   ] cents (give your answer to the nearest cent).

12.8 Company C has just announced that its dividend per share for the previous year was $0.40. C maintains a dividend payout ratio of 50%.

C is all-equity financed, and finances new investments from retained earnings. C invests its retained earnings and estimates that they will deliver a return on equity of 10% per annum.

C's cost of capital is 8%.

What is the estimated value of C's shares?

$ [_____] (Give your answer to the nearest whole $.)

12.9 GER Co had a cost of equity of 14%. As a result of an issue of debentures to finance the replacement of obsolete equipment, the cost of equity has gone up to 15%.

GER is not in a tax-paying position, and its weighted average cost of capital has not changed as a result of the debenture issue.

All other things being equal, the share price is MOST likely to?

O   Stay the same

O   Increase

O   Decrease

O   Need more information

12.10 The following figures are taken from the income statement of Company G for the year ended 30 September 20X4.

	$m
Profit before interest and tax	45
Depreciation	5
Dividend to ordinary shareholders	1
Interest paid	4
Tax	12

In addition G spent $20 million on tangible assets to replace existing obsolete assets. G's working capital increased by $3 million during the year ended 30 September 20X4.

Calculate Company G's cash flow to equity for the year ended 30 September 20X4.

$ [_____] million

12.11 An investor makes all his investment decisions just by analysing historical share price movements and expects to beat the market by predicting future price changes.

What type of stock market efficiency is the investor assuming?

O   Weak form efficiency

O   Semi-strong form efficiency

O   Strong form efficiency

O   No efficiency at all

12.12 Company A is a supplier to high-class restaurants; it is a profitable, high-growth company – as reflected in its P/E ratio of 15.

The directors of Company A are considering the acquisition of Company B, a rival company that has been underperforming in recent years. Company B's profits before tax have been constant at around $400,000.

Company B has an estimated cost of equity of 10%, and pays out all of its earnings as a dividend.

The tax rate is 28%.

Which of the following is the BEST estimate of the value of Company B under Company A's ownership?

○ $6m

○ $2.88m

○ $4m

○ $4.32m

12.13 Company VX is considering making a bid for Company Z.

Company Z is a listed company with 250 million shares in issue.

Company VX has an established a range of values for Company Z as follows:

Book value of net assets $700 million

Realisable value of net assets $800 million

Earnings valuation applied to forecast earnings $1,050 million

Market capitalisation $1,000 million

What is the minimum share price VX should offer to Z's shareholders?

[   ] per share (give your answer to the nearest whole $).

12.14 A company has $50 million (nominal or par value) of $0.50 ordinary shares in issue with a market price of $2.00.

A proposed new project requires an initial investment of $10 million which will be financed by the company's existing cash holdings.

The project's inflows are expected to be worth $15 million in present value terms.

Assume the market is semi-strong form efficient and the share price moves to reflect this information on the day the project is announced.

What is the theoretical movement in the share price on that day?

○ No change

○ $0.05 increase

○ $0.10 increase

○ $0.15 increase

12.15 BR Co's dividend payments per share over the last few years have been as follows.

	$
20X0	0.65
20X1	0.69
20X2	0.72
20X3	0.80
20X4	0.92

The dividend for 20X4 has just been paid. The company's cost of equity is 12%.

What is the estimated value of a share in BR using the dividend growth model?

O $31.72

O $34.61

O $7.67

O $20.55

12.16 Company C is using the calculated intangible value (CIV) company valuation method to value its intangible assets.

Relevant data:

- Company C has a WACC of 10%, cost of debt of 8% and cost of equity of 12%
- Company C's tangible assets are $60 million
- Average profit before tax for Company C is $80 million
- Industry average return on tangible assets is 11%
- Corporate income tax is 35%

Complete the following CIV calculation using the picklist options below.

CIV = [$80 million – (11% × $60 million)] × [　　　　▼] / [　　　　▼]

Picklist:
0.10
0.08
1.10
1.12
0.35
0.65

12.17 An unlisted manufacturer of orchestral musical instruments is a substantial operator in the market and has a solid reputation as a dependable manufacturer. Last year the company made operating profits of $22 million.

The average P/E ratio in the stock market is 10, and the average for musical instrument manufacturers is 8.

The company pays tax at 20% and has an $18 million (nominal value) of undated 6% bonds in issue trading at $17 million.

What is the BEST estimate of the value of the company's equity?

O $134 million

O $220 million

O $167 million

O $176 million

BPP
LEARNING
MEDIA

12.18 Company A has prepared a valuation of a competitor company, Company B. Company A is intending to acquire a controlling interest in the equity of Company B and therefore wants to value only the equity of Company B. The directors of Company A have prepared the following valuation of Company B:

	Year 1 $ million	Year 2 $ million	Year 3 onwards $ million
Forecast free cash flow to all investors	10	12	14
Discount factor @ 8%	0.926	0.857	0.794
Present value	9.26	10.28	11.12

Value of equity = 9.26 + 10.28 + 11.12 = $30.66 million

The following information is relevant to Company B:

Tax rate	20%
Cost of equity	10%
WACC	8%
Debt finance	$10 million 5% undated bonds.

Which THREE of the following are weaknesses of the above valuation?

☐ The valuation is understated as forecast future growth has been ignored beyond Year 3.

☐ The valuation is overstated as the directors have failed to deduct tax from the free cash flows.

☐ The valuation is understated as the directors have failed to include a perpetuity factor in the calculations.

☐ Free cash flows to all investors should be discounted at 10% being the cost of equity and not 8% being WACC.

☐ The approach used calculates the value of the total entity not the value of equity.

12.19 A is an unlisted professional training company owned by its two founding directors; it operates in a niche market specialising in a particular area of health care training. It has experienced extremely high growth over the last two years. Although market growth is expected to continue, it is expected at a much lower rate. A employs a number of health care trainers who are highly regarded in the market and are key to its success. A has recently been approached by a private equity firm as an acquisition target. The directors of A wish to establish the value of the company to use in negotiations with private equity firm. They have decided to use the price-earnings (P/E) method and have prepared a draft valuation.

The following information is relevant:

Industry average P/E 10

A's operating profit £320,000

A's profit for the year £200,000

Draft valuation of A prepared by the directors:

Value of A = 10 × £320,000 = £3,200,000

Which THREE of the following are weaknesses in the above valuation of A?

☐ The profit figure ignores the intangible value attached to A's employees.

☐ The industry average P/E ratio should not be used in these circumstances.

☐ The use of operating profit is incorrect.

☐ The valuation fails to take account of any expected future growth in the market.

☐ Current year profit is unlikely to reflect sustainable earnings.

12.20 Company X is a leading developer of computer games. Company X's success is attributable to the high calibre games writers it employs. Company X would like to establish a valuation of the company, including its intellectual capital. The following information is relevant:

Company X's value of tangible assets	$15 million
Company X's most recent profit before tax	$3 million
Average return on tangible assets for game developing companies	10%
Company B's cost of capital	8%
Corporate income tax rate	20%

What is the value of Company X using the CIV approach?

O $28.75 million

O $15.00 million

O $30.00 million

O $18.75 million

---

13 Advanced valuation methods

13.1 It is currently 20X6, estimates for inflation for the next three years are given below:

	UK	USA
20X7	3%	4%
20X8	2%	5%
20X9	2%	3.5%

The current spot rate (20X6) is 0.5 GBP (£) to the USD ($).

Using purchasing power parity theory, what is the forecast USD/GBP ($/£) exchange rate for the end of 20X9?

O 0.527 USD/GBP

O 0.535 USD/GBP

O 0.474 USD/GBP

O 0.493 USD/GBP

13.2 A treaty between two governments whereby tax payable on profits made by an overseas subsidiary may be deductible against tax on the same profits in another country.

This definition describes which of the following?

○   Double tax agreement

○   Tax authority clearance

○   Government incentive

○   Withholding tax

13.3 **Which of the following is/are correct in relation to the effect of the purchasing power parity theory on exchange rates?**

Select ALL that apply.

☐   If prices are rising faster in Country C than in Country D, the currency of Country C will weaken against that of Country D.

☐   If prices are rising slower in Country D than in Country E and in Country F, Country D's currency will strengthen against those of Countries E and F.

☐   Inflation in the UK is expected to be 2.5% and 3.3% in the USA. If today's exchange rate is $1.42 = £1 the expected exchange rate in one year is $1.4311 = £1.

☐   Inflation in the UK is expected to be 2.5% and 3.3% in the USA. If today's exchange rate is $1.42 = £1 the expected exchange rate in one year is $1.4090 = £1.

13.4 The following information is relevant:

	Country Y	Country S
Real interest rate	2%	3%
Inflation rate	3%	5%
Currency	Y$	S$

The current spot rate is Y$/S$ 2.32 (that is 2.32S$ to 1Y$)

Using interest rate parity theory, what is the forecast Y$/S$ exchange rate in one years' time?

Year 1 [   ] to two decimal places.

13.5 **Which of the following BEST describes the effect of the purchasing power parity theory?**

○   When interest rates in Country A are higher than in Country B, the currency of Country A will depreciate against that of Country B.

○   When inflation rates in Country A are higher than in Country B, the currency of Country A will depreciate against that of Country B.

○   When interest rates in Country A are lower than in Country B, the currency of Country A will depreciate against that of Country B.

○   When inflation rates in Country A are lower than in Country B, the currency of Country A will depreciate against that of Country B.

13.6 **Match the following terms to their definitions.**

A treaty between two governments whereby tax payable on profits made by an overseas subsidiary may be deductible against tax on the same profits in another country

[▼]

A local tax on remittances paid to an overseas investor – normally applied to interest and dividend payments

[▼]

A mechanism triggered by a serious takeover bid whereby the shares become more difficult to acquire

[▼]

Picklist:

Withholding tax
Corporate tax agreement
Poison pill
Double tax agreement

13.7 In the country of Utopia the currency is the Utopian pound (£) and in Dystopia the currency is the Dystopian dollar ($).

The current spot rate is 1.05 $/£ (that is £1.05 = $1).

Inflation in Utopia is 3.2% and in Dystopia it is 6.8%. Based on this information the $/£ exchange rate in exactly one year will be:

[   ] to four decimal places.

13.8

	$ million
Operating profit	400
Depreciation and amortisation	140
Finance charges	30
Capital expenditure to sustain operations	180
Tax	90
Repayment of borrowings	100
Equity dividend	60

What is the BEST estimate of cash flow to equity?

O $80 million

O $140 million

O $180 million

O $240 million

13.9   HAM is a company based in the Eurozone and whose base currency is the euro. It is planning to acquire the entire share capital of a company called DUF which is based in the USA and whose base currency is the US Dollar ($). A cash flow valuation is being prepared for the acquisition.

Inflation in the Eurozone is expected to be 5% and 2% in the USA for the foreseeable future.

All other things being equal what impact will the expected exchange rate movement have on the euro-denominated valuation of Company DUF today?

○   No impact

○   Increase

○   Decrease

○   There is no expected exchange rate movement

13.10   Z is a parent company whose functional currency is the Z$.

Z has a foreign subsidiary, G, which is located in Country G and has the G$ as its functional currency.

The exchange rate is G$1:Z$2 and this is not expected to change in the near future.

G Co has G$5 million of surplus cash which Z wishes to use to pay a special dividend.

G has already paid 20% corporation tax on profits and would need to pay withholding tax of 10% on any cash remitted to Z. Z would pay tax of 15% on cash received from G.

The maximum special dividend that could be paid by Z, using funds from G, is approximately which of the following?

○   Special dividend Z$0.68 million (G$5 million × 80% × 10% × 200% × 85%)

○   Special dividend Z$7.65 million (G$5 million × 90% × 85% × 200%)

○   Special dividend Z$1.91 million (G$5 million × 90% × 85% × 50%)

○   Special dividend Z$6.12 million (G$5 million × 80% × 90% × 85% × 200%)

13.11   **Match the following valuation approaches to their definitions:**

Next year's expected dividend discounted as a perpetuity using the difference between cost of equity and anticipated growth as the discount rate	[▼]
Cash generated by the company after tax, reinvestment needs and debt related cash flows discounted at the cost of equity	[▼]
Cash generated by the company after tax, and investment needs but before debt related cash flows discounted at the weighted average cost of capital less the value of debt	[▼]

Picklist:

Cash flow to all investors valuation
Cash flow to equity valuation
Dividend valuation based on constant dividend growth
Dividend valuation based on constant dividends

13.12 Company A, a conglomerate company, intends to use a cash flow approach to value an Australian newspaper publishing subsidiary which it intends to dispose of.

As part of this process, Company A intends to use a proxy company to derive an appropriate cost of capital for valuing the subsidiary company.

Which of the following characteristics of the proxy company should be the same as the subsidiary company?

O   Company size

O   Industry

O   Gearing

O   Country

13.13 X is a car manufacturer based in Country X, where the local currency is the X$.

In two years time X plans to sell an overseas subsidiary whose currency is the Z$ for an estimated Z$400m.

The Z$/X$ spot rate is Z$ 1 = X$ 1.5400. Interest rates per year for the next two years are forecast to be:

- Z$ interest rate 4% per year
- X$ interest rate 2% per year

Using this data, what is the BEST estimate of the X$ value that X will obtain in two years' time?

O   X$593m

O   X$640m

O   X$265m

O   X$270m

13.14 Company A operates in Country A with the A$ as its currency. It is looking to acquire Company B who operates in Country B with the B$ as its currency.

The following information is relevant:

Current exchange rate	B$1 = A$ 0.5
Rate of inflation in Country A	2%
Rate of inflation in Country B	4%
Company A's WACC	6%
Company A's cost of equity	8%

Company A has prepared the following valuation of Company B's equity. However, there are some errors in the calculations.

	Year 1	Year 2	Year 3 and each year thereafter
Forecast free cash flow to all investors B$ million	100	110	120
Forecast exchange rate	0.5098	0.5198	0.5300
Forecast free cash flow to all investors A$ million	50.98	57.18	63.60
Discount factor @ 6%	0.943	0.890	0.840
Present value A$ million	48.07	50.89	53.42

Value of Company B's equity = 48.07 + 50.89 + 53.42 = A$152.38 million Company B has B$10 million of debt finance.

BPP
LEARNING
MEDIA

Which of the following THREE statements are true?

☐ The calculations show Company B's entity value, not its equity value.

☐ The valuation is understated as forecast future growth has been ignored beyond Year 3.

☐ The forecast exchange rates are incorrect as they show the B$ strengthening and it should be weakening

☐ The conversion into A$ is incorrect as the assistant should have divided by the exchange rate and not multiplied.

☐ Cash flow to all investors should be discounted at 8% being the company's cost of equity and not 6% being WACC.

13.15   A is an unlisted company, funded by a mixture of debt and equity.

B is a listed company and operates in the same market as A. B has no debt.

No cost of equity has been calculated for A.

Which of the following is the MOST appropriate method for valuing the equity of A?

○ Use the cost of equity of B, adjusted for gearing, as a proxy to derive the weighted average cost of capital for A and apply it to A's cash flow to all investors.

○ Use the cost of equity of B, adjusted for gearing, as a proxy to derive the cost of equity for A and apply it to A's cash flow to all investors.

○ Use the cost of equity of B, adjusted for gearing, as a proxy to derive the weighted average cost of capital for A and apply it to A's cash flow to all investors, then deduct the value of A's debt.

○ Use the cost of equity of B, adjusted for gearing, as a proxy to derive the cost of equity for A and apply it to A's cash flow to all investors, then deduct the value of A's debt.

13.16   Company A is an unlisted company. The following information is relevant to Company A:

- It has bank borrowings of $50 million.
- It has $100 million of equity finance.

Company B is a listed company with $50 million of debt and 50 million shares with a share price of $4.

Company B has an equity beta of 1.6 and the beta of debt can be assumed to be zero.

The rate of corporate income tax applicable to both companies is 20%.

The risk-free rate is 4% and the market return is 10%.

What is the cost of equity of company A?

[   ] % to one decimal place.

13.17 Company A is a listed company with $400 million of capital (using market values) of which $100 million is debt.

Company A has an asset beta of 1.2 and a debt beta of 0.3.

The risk-free rate is 4% and the equity risk premium is 8%.

Corporation tax is 20%.

What is the estimated cost of equity for Company A?

[   ] % to one decimal place.

14 Pricing and post-transaction issues

14.1 In the context of company restructuring, what is a spin-off?

○ The offering of one new free share for every share currently held

○ The sale of part of a company to a third party

○ The creation of a new company, where the shareholders of the original company own the shares

○ The purchase of all or part of the company by its managers

14.2 **Which THREE of the following statements describe the concept of bootstrapping in the context of an acquisition?**

☐ A high growth company is acquiring a lower growth company in the same sector on the assumption that the acquiring company would be able to turn the target company's fortunes around.

☐ The acquisition of a company with a lower price–earnings ratio allows the acquiring company to create a higher EPS and share price for its shareholders.

☐ The acquisition of a company with a lower share price in the hope that the share price will average out with that of the acquiring company.

☐ The acquisition of a company in the same sector in order to benefit from advantageous tax treatment and other financial advantages.

☐ The acquisition of a company in the same industry sector and the value of the acquisition is determined by whether the target company achieves predetermined performance targets.

☐ The post-acquisition value of the combined entity will be equal to the acquiring company's P/E ratio multiplied by the combined earnings of the two companies.

14.3 **Which of the following is LEAST likely to be an advantage of a management buy-out (MBO) as a means of disposing of a business?**

○ Greater degree of co-operation from divisional managers in the completion of the acquisition

○ Less likely to attract the attention of the competition authorities

○ Greater personal motivation and quicker decision making once the MBO is complete

○ The managers leading the MBO do not need to invest personally in order to obtain finance from venture capitalists

14.4 The directors of Alpha Co wish to dispose of one of its subsidiaries, Beta Co.

Beta Co is going through a phase of rapid expansion. The directors of Beta Co are interested in a management buy-out (MBO) of Beta Co.

There is a potential conflict of interest if, during the negotiation phase of the MBO, the directors of Beta Co were to:

○ Employ more sales staff in Beta's sales office

○ Delay projects with an internal rate of return that is above Beta's cost of capital.

○ Revalue Beta's assets

○ Sell and leaseback buildings that Beta uses

14.5 Company F is considering making an offer for the entire share capital of Company N. The offer will be a cash offer financed by raising new debt.

	Company F	Company N
EPS	$1.25	$3.50
P/E ratio	14.0	9.2
Number of shares	15 million	2.5 million

Assuming a full bootstrapping effect, calculate the estimated share price of the merged entity.

○ $19.60

○ $22.00

○ $24.85

○ $25.67

14.6 Company H is considering launching a bid to acquire the entire share capital of Company S by paying a 20% premium above the current share price.

The offer will be a share exchange. The following data is relevant to the bid.

	Company H	Company S
Share price	$24	$4
Number of shares	200 million	150 million

How many shares must Company H offer to the shareholders of Company S?

[   ] million (to the nearest million)

14.7 Company DEF is about to launch a bid to acquire the share capital of Company GHI, which is of a similar size to Company DEF. The bid will be a cash bid. DEF shareholders have indicated that they are not willing to invest any further funds in Company DEF and a new issue of shares to new shareholders is unlikely to happen. There is no earn-out arrangement.

DEF currently does not have sufficient cash flows to purchase GHI.

Which THREE of the following are likely to result from the cash bid?

☐ DEF's gearing will increase.

☐ There will be a dilution of DEF's shareholders' control.

☐ Risk in connection with the future performance of GHI is shared between both sets of shareholders.

☐ The number of shares in issue will increase.

☐ The GHI shareholders may be taxed on any gain on the shares depending on what kind of shareholder they are.

☐ DEF's cost of equity will increase.

14.8 Company P has a market value as a standalone company of $450 million.

Company T has a market value as a standalone company of $150 million.

Company P is to acquire Company T for $160 million. The consideration will be in the form of Company P ordinary share capital.

Sales synergies of $10 million per year and cost synergies of $7 million per year are expected indefinitely.

Assume a cost of capital of 10% and ignore any tax impact.

What is the impact of the acquisition on the original Company P shareholders' wealth?

○ Decrease of $10 million

○ Increase of $20 million

○ Increase of $160 million

○ Increase of $170 million

14.9 Company JMU is about to bid for the entire share capital of Company BHA.

The bid will offer two JMU shares for seven of Company BHA's shares.

	Company JMU	Company BHA
Number of shares (pre-acquisition)	100 million	210 million
Earnings per share	$2.00	$0.95
P/E ratio	12	9

In order to achieve a post-merger share price of $26.75, what is the present value of any synergies needed?

$ [   ] million (give answer to the nearest $0.1 million).

BPP
LEARNING
MEDIA

Which THREE of the following are objectives of a post-audit in connection with an acquisition?

☐ To ensure the acquisition target's accounts present a true and fair view of its financial performance and position

☐ To ensure there are no hidden risks in connection with the acquisition

☐ To undertake an independent investigation into whether the acquisition has achieved its aims

☐ To provide some organisational experience and learning so that future acquisitions are successfully executed

☐ To give assurance that the synergy forecasts are realistic

14.11 Company HVS is an all equity financed company. It has recently made an acquisition of a smaller company and the combined earnings are $300 million per annum and a cost of equity of 12%. The company pays tax at 20% of its taxable profits. Following the acquisition the directors have decided to increase the company's gearing permanently by borrowing $500 million undated debt at an interest rate of 6% per annum pre-tax.

Based on Modigliani and Miller's theory what is the value of Company HVS's equity?

O $2,100 million

O $2,500 million

O $2,600 million

O $3,000 million

14.12 **Which of the following is MOST likely to be successfully used as a post-bid defence against a hostile takeover?**

O Declaration of a special dividend

O Issue of convertible preference shares that can be converted on favourable terms if there is change of ownership

O Change articles of association to increase the percentage of shareholders that are needed to approve a takeover bid

O White knight strategy

14.13 C Co is planning the acquisition of E Co, one of its key rivals. The following information is available:

	C Co	E Co
NPV of cash flows pre-acquisition ($m)	100	80
NPV post acquisition	195	n/a

The maximum price that C Co should offer for the equity of E Co is:

$ [   ] million

14.14   XX is valuing a potential acquisition target, Company YY, which operates in the same industry as XX.

XX is intending to use a bootstrapping approach for this valuation.

Which of the following would be used in this approach.

Select ALL that apply.

☐   XX's earnings in $m

☐   YY's earnings in $m

☐   XX's P/E ratio

☐   YY's P/E ratio

☐   XX's cost of equity

14.15   ED Co is a large energy company specialising in nuclear power. ED wishes to acquire company BN Co which is in the same sector but based in a neighbouring country. BN is about half the size of ED.

ED is considering how best to structure the bid offer. ED currently has 50% gearing (debt/debt + equity) and is considering funding a cash offer partly financed by raising additional debt finance (20%) and partly financed from existing reserves (80%).

Using a cash bid as opposed to a share exchange is MOST likely to have the effect of:

○   Diluting ED's shareholder control

○   Lowering ED's gearing

○   Reducing ED's dividends per share

○   Increasing ED's EPS

14.16   A company is financed by a combination of equity valued at $100 million and debt capital valued at $50 million. The rate of tax is 30%.

According to Modigliani and Miller, what would be the total market value of a company identical in every respect, except that it is all-equity financed?

The value of an identical all-equity company would be:

$ [   ] million

14.17   A large logistics company, Statex Co, is interested in acquiring a smaller logistics company called Direct Parcels (DP). DP made profits before tax of $750,000 in the latest financial year.

Information on potential P/E ratios to use to value DP is given below:

- Average P/E ratio for listed companies = 13
- Average P/E for logistics companies = 8
- Average P/E for recently acquired logistics companies = 10

The corporate tax rate is 25%.

Using the above information, what is the MOST appropriate value of DP?

- ○ $4.500m
- ○ $5.625m
- ○ $7.3125m
- ○ $7.500m

14.18   Fenton Co is preparing to acquire Stork Co in a 1 for 2 share for share exchange.

Fenton Co currently has 100 million shares in issue, valued at $4 per share and Stork Co has 40 million shares in issue, valued at $2 per share.

Synergies of $5 million per annum pre-tax are expected to be generated by the takeover as a perpetuity.

The post-acquisition cost of equity is estimated to be 10%.

The corporate tax rate is 20%.

What is the likely share price of Fenton Co after the acquisition?

- ○ $4.33
- ○ $4.42
- ○ $3.25
- ○ $3.31

14.19   Company A is a software development company. It was established five years ago and grew rapidly in the first three years due to the combined efforts of its founding directors and strong management team. The company has untapped potential and needs new investment to realise this. As a result, earnings growth has flattened out in the last 12 months. Despite its success, the company is not yet sufficiently large enough to obtain a listing on the local stock exchange.

The two founding directors, who own 100% of the company, are happy with its success and are now considering different strategies that would enable them to realise the full value of their current investment. They have identified a new investment opportunity and therefore need to realise the full value of their investment in Company A immediately to enable them to raise finance for the new venture.

Which THREE of the following exit strategies could the directors of Company A consider?

- ☐   Earn-out arrangement
- ☐   Trade sale
- ☐   Private equity buy-in
- ☐   Management buyout (MBO)
- ☐   Initial public offering (IPO)

14.20 Portas Co is a successful global sportswear manufacturer. It has identified a smaller national sportswear manufacturer Tribal Co as a potential takeover target. Synergistic benefits from the merger would result in an increase in after-tax earnings of $45 million per year.

Portas Co has made an offer of two of its shares for every one of Tribal Co.

Information from the latest financial statements for both companies is shown below:

	Portas Co	Tribal Co
Profit after tax	$200 million	$80 million
Number of shares	4000 million	500 million
Market price of shares	100c	250c

After the takeover, the price of Portas shares rose by 36.5c.

What is the implied P/E ratio of the group?

| | to one decimal place.

Answers to objective test questions

1 Strategic objectives

1.1 The correct answer is: **$700,000.**

The profit figure to be used for the calculation of EPS is the profit after tax, and after deducting preferred dividends. In this case the calculation is $950,000, less $50,000 interest, less $100,000 tax, less $100,000 preferred dividend.

1.2 The correct answer is: **32%**

Current share price = P/E × EPS = 13 × 0.25 = 3.25

Previous share price = 12.5 × 0.2 = 2.5

Capital gain = 3.25 – 2.5 = 0.75 per share

Current dividend = 0.05

Total share holder return = (dividend + capital gain) / opening share price

= (0.05 + 0.75) / 2.5 × 100 = 32%

1.3 The correct answer is: **7%**

The dividend yield is calculated as the ordinary dividend per share divided by the market price per share.

Here, the ordinary dividend per share is $0.5m / 3.5 million shares = $0.143. So dividend yield = 0.143 / share price of $2 = 0.07 or 7%.

The other (incorrect) answers are obtained if you use the total dividend (ordinary + preference) or if you use 7 million shares instead of 3.5 million. The latter is an understandable error because the shares have a nominal value of $0.5 / share, but the question does state that there are 3.5 million shares in issue so no adjustment is needed.

1.4 The correct answer is: **2.51, debt covenant is not broken.**

Operating profit will increase by	=	$18,000
Interest payable will increase by	=	$140,000 × 5%
	=	$7,000
Interest cover	=	PBIT/Interest payable
	=	$118,000/$47,000
	=	2.51

This is above the covenant of 2.2 so the covenant is not broken.

Note that you may have calculated interest cover of 2.95 if you ignored the increase in interest from the new loan.

Interest cover of approximately 1.06 results from incorrectly using profits after tax in the interest cover calculation.

1.5 The incorrect definition is: **Efficiency means doing things quickly: minimising the amount of time that is spent on a given activity.**

Efficiency does not mean doing things quickly. It means doing things well and getting the best use out of the money spent. Efficiency can be measured as the input/output ratio for any process or activity.

All the other definitions are correct for a not-for-profit organisation.

1.6   The correct answers are:

- Cost per student of providing tuition.
- Cash deficit avoided.
- Student achievement level.

The first two measures are focused on economy and efficiency, achievement level is an effectiveness measure (clearly if students are not achieving then the course is ineffective).

The number of students enrolling is outside the control of the college – it would be of interest in a value for money review but is not directly controllable by the college and is also indirectly measured by the cash deficit measure.

Satisfaction with facilities is again of some interest but is of a lower level of importance because facilities are only one aspect that affects overall student satisfaction.

1.7   The correct answer is: **To maximise the wealth of its ordinary shareholders.**

Whether listed or not, this is the **primary** financial objective.

Even for an unlisted company, wealth for shareholders can come in two forms; either from increasing the capital growth of the shares they own or increasing the dividend that is paid out annually to shareholders.

All of the other objectives are **secondary** objectives.

1.8   The correct answers are:

- **The primary objective of Entity A will be to maximise shareholder wealth.**

- **The managers of Entity B are likely to have very little input or choice over its objectives.**

- **Entity B will have to demonstrate value for money.**

Entity A is publicly listed so its main objective will be the maximisation of shareholder wealth.

Entity B is state owned so it will have to demonstrate value for money (and its managers will have little if any control over this) and its objectives are also likely to relate to a level of service. Entity B will have financial objectives as part its economy and efficiency measures.

1.9   The correct answers are:

- EPS = 12.5c.
- P/E multiple = 24.

Earnings = turnover – operating costs – interest – tax = $125 million

No. shares = 1,000 million

So EPS = 125/1000 = $0.125 or 12.5c

P/E = 300/12.5 = 24

1.10   The correct answer is: **Interest cover is 7 and the existing covenant will not be breached.**

X's profits before interest and tax is the profit before tax figure of $81 million with the existing interest of $10 million ($200 million × 0.05) added back, ie $91 million.

Interest cover is PBIT/interest so this is $91 divided by the current interest figure of $10 million plus the new interest payable of $3 million (0.06 × $50 million). So this is 91/13 = 7.

This is above the covenant of 6 so the covenant has not been breached.

1.11   The correct answer is: **14%**

$$\sqrt[4]{\frac{34}{20}} - 1 = 14.2\%$$ which is 14% to the nearest whole percentage point.

The number of time periods = 4 as there are four growth periods (even though there are five years).

1.12   The correct answer is: **W$144,000.**

	Year 1
	W$'000
Revenue	1,800
Cost of sales	1,080
Gross profit	720
Operating expenses	400
PBIT	320
Interest	140
PBT	180
Tax @ 20%	36
PAT	144

$176,000 incorrectly applies the 10% reduction to operating expenses too.

$48,000 only applies the 10% reduction to salves revenue and not cost of sales.

$240,000 incorrectly applies the 10% reduction to operating expenses too and does not account for the increase in the interest rates.

1.13   The correct answer is: **16%**

20X2 DPS = $50 million/10 million = $10

20X6 DPS = $108 million/6 million = $18

Therefore the growth rate is 4 (18/10) = 15.8% being 16% to the nearest whole percentage.

1.14   The correct answer is: **Manufactured capital.**

This is defined by the IIRC as 'manufactured physical objects available for use in the production of goods or the provision of services, including buildings, equipment and infrastructure'.

Financial capital is 'the pool of funds that is available to an organisation for use in the production of goods or services and obtained through financing, such as debt, equity or grants, or generated through operations or investments'.

Natural capital is 'renewable and non-renewable environmental resources and processes including air, water, land, minerals, forests, bio-diversity and eco-system health'.

Social and relationship capital is 'the institutions and relationships within and between communities, groups of stakeholders and other networks, and the ability to share information to enhance individual and collective well-being'.

1.15 The correct answers are:

- The market would become aware of the investment SR has made in its employees which would create greater market confidence in SR and potentially result in an increase in share price.

- Employees would feel more valued and potentially work harder generating additional profit for SR.

- It would help improve staff retention and would attract potential new high quality employees to the company generating increased return for investors through retaining and recruiting talent.

Comprehensive disclosure would have no impact on the audit report as the audit opinion only covers the financial statements and notes to the accounts. Extra voluntary disclosure such as a management commentary or sustainability report are not required to be audited although an entity might choose to contract a reporting accountant to provide an opinion on their sustainability report.

The time and cost of producing narrative disclosures and the adverse impact on profitability would be a **disadvantage**, not an advantage to investors.

Whilst voluntary narrative disclosures might make it easier for SR to raise finance in the future, this is an advantage to SR not the investors.

2 Strategic financial policy decisions

2.1 The correct answers are:

- Planning and obtaining suitable sources of finance.
- Generating and evaluating investment proposals.

In the early stages of an entity's life, and often beyond, cash flow management is critical so planning appropriate sources of finance is critical to ensure the survival of the entity.

Investment planning will always be vital for generating shareholder wealth, but this is often especially important in the early years of an entity's life where failure to invest appropriately can cause the entity to fail.

Dividends are unlikely to be paid in the early years of an entity's life due to the need to invest and the importance of managing cash flow. So this is unlikely to be a focus of time and effort for financial decision-making at this stage of an entity's life cycle.

Social and environmental reporting may be important for some entities but looks less important in terms of financial decision-making than the other issues here.

2.2 The correct answer is: **No impact.**

The project will be rejected so the cash flows of the company will be unaffected.

2.3 The correct answers are:

- High-growth companies are likely to need high levels of capital investment, use low levels of debt finance and retain high proportions of profits rather than pay out dividends.

- Mature companies tend not to require high levels of capital investment, they use high levels of debt and make high dividend payouts.

In summary:

Decision	High-growth companies	Mature companies
Investment	High	Moderate/low
Financing (use of debt)	Low	High
Dividend	Low/zero	High

2.4   The correct answer is: **Dividend yield.**

The formula is simplified to Dividend per share ÷ Share price.

EPS × Dividend payout = Dividend per share

EPS × P/E = Share price

Dividend per share / share price = Dividend yield

2.5   The correct answer is: **59.4 cents**

The share price is P/E × EPS = 22 × 45 cents = 990 cents

The dividend per share is 6% of the share price = 6% × 990 cents = 59.4 cents

2.6   The correct answers are:

	True	False
Using a loan sourced in an overseas country can be an effective way to manage translation and political risk.	✓	☐
High-growth companies are inherently risky because of the speed of their transformation as they grow so they usually require low levels of debt and high dividend payout ratios.	☐	✓
Withholding tax increases the political risk associated with making investments overseas.	✓	☐

Gains or losses on the retranslation of overseas assets into the domestic currency is offset by gains or losses on the translation of the loan. In the event of forced withdrawal from a country, the company can default on the loan.

High-growth companies need low dividend payout ratios in order to maintain liquidity (speculative motive).

Political risk is the risk associated with government action or that of other political agents. Witholding tax can serve as a restriction on the movement of dividends from one country to another and is usually controlled by governments.

2.7   The correct answer is: **No, the overdraft facility would be exceeded by approximately $360,000.**

	$'000	
Revenue	17,200	
Purchases	(8,400)	assuming no credit
Opening payables	(2,754)	(8400 × 60/183)
Other costs	(8,000)	
b/f	(200)	
	(2,154)	
	354	over the overdraft limit of 1,800

2.8   The correct answers are:

- **Investment in projects with a positive NPV.**
- **Enhanced brand reputation and recognition.**
- **Moving profitable operations to low-tax regimes.**

Each of these is likely to enhance the present value of an entity's future cash flows.

Directors bonuses do not in themselves bring any direct benefit to shareholders.

Increasing the rate of dividend growth MAY lead to an entity being starved of funds for re-investment.

BPP
LEARNING
MEDIA

2.9　The correct answer is: **The company's dividend is 15.4 cents per share and its share price is 462.0 cents per share.**

Dividend is 40% × 38.5 cents = 15.4 cents

Share price = EPS × PE ratio = 38.5 cents × 12 = 462.0 cents

2.10　The correct answers are:

	True	False
A company that increases its profit will always see an increase in its share price as a result.		✓
A key consideration in the financing decision is to maximise the cost of capital.		✓
Keeping surplus cash in order to pay a larger than usual tax liability in three months is an example of the speculative motive.		✓

A company's share price is likely to be a function of future expectations rather than the historical profitability.

Although it is not the only consideration the cost of capital is a key consideration. However it is usual to try to minimise it rather than maximise it.

The speculative motive suggests that companies keep surplus cash in order to exploit wealth creating opportunities. This is not the case here.

3　Long-term debt finance

3.1　The correct answers are:

	True	False
Unsecured bonds are likely to require a higher yield to maturity than equivalent secured bonds	✓	
Convertible bonds give the borrower the right but not the obligation to turn the bond into a predetermined number of ordinary shares		✓
A Eurobond is a bond that is denominated in a currency which is not native to where the bond itself is issued	✓	

Unsecured bonds are more risky for the lender. For that reason the lender will generally require a higher return on their investment to compensate for their risk.

Convertibles give the lender or investor (not the borrower) the right to convert the bond into shares.

A Eurobond is a bond in a currency which is not that of the country of issue. For example, if a British company issued a US Dollar bond in the UK, this would be a Eurobond.

3.2　The correct answer is: **Annual interest received as a % of the nominal value of the bond.**

The coupon rate is the interest stated in the bond documentation, and is (normally) based on the **nominal value** of the bond, ie a 5% bond pays 5% of the nominal value – here the coupon rate is 5%.

The return as a percent of the ex-interest market price is called **interest yield**. The return that takes into account capital repayment is called **redemption yield**.

3.3   The correct answers are:

	True	False
On conversion date, the ordinary shareholders of the company have the option to choose whether or not the bonds should be converted into shares.	☐	☑
The bondholder can normally claim tax relief on interest paid on the bond up to conversion.	☐	☑

With convertible bonds it is the **bondholders** who have the right to choose whether or not to convert their bondholding into shares.

The **company** can claim tax relief, not the bondholder.

3.4   The correct answer is: **An undertaking by a company to a lender to keep dividend payments within a specified limit.**

A loan agreement or bond issuance agreement might include a covenant on dividend restraint. This would be an undertaking by the company to restrict dividends in a specified way as long as the loan or debt remains outstanding.

A company cannot pay dividends until interest payment obligations are met for legal reasons that are not connected to this type of covenant.

A company cannot pay dividends if it cannot raise the cash to do this; again this is not connected to this type of covenant.

3.5   The correct answer is: **A lease.**

This will give predictability to S's cash outflows, and this is likely to be an issue for a newly formed company in an unstable market. Also a debt covenant will not be imposed.

A floating-rate bank loan is incorrect because it would expose S to high levels of interest rate risk which is undesirable given the challenge of meeting the net debt to EBITDA target.

A revolving credit facility is incorrect because flexibility to change the amount of finance that it requires does not appear to be a key issue here. This is also a source of short-term finance which would be inappropriate for an investment in a long-term asset.

A bond issue is incorrect because it is unlikely to be feasible for a small, recently established unlisted company.

3.6   The correct answer is: **Leasing.**

Retained earnings are not a source of debt finance, and we are told that Xpat is looking to use debt finance.

Convertibles would be unlikely for an unlisted company.

Eurobonds denominated in US $ would introduce unnecessary FX risk to the company. IRP would mean that any gains made on the interest rate would be offset against the exchange rate. Also, a Eurobond issue is unlikely unless the company is a multinational.

Leasing seems appropriate given the nature of the business; new sites could be leased instead of being purchased.

3.7   The correct answer: **$210 million.**

$10 million is just the interest payment and incorrectly excludes the redemption.

31 December 20X2 is the date of redemption – so the nominal value of $200 million will be repaid **plus** the final interest repayment of $10 million. $210 million is the correct answer.

$220 million is wrong as an answer because it is based on the market value of the bond ($210 million) – in fact it is the book value that is repaid at the redemption date plus interest of $10 million.

$200 million is wrong as it is just the redemption value and incorrectly excludes the interest payment due.

BPP
LEARNING
MEDIA

3.8   The correct answers are:

	True	False
Deep discounted bonds always have a lower market value than nominal value and sometimes have a lower coupon rate than other bonds with similar risk profile.	☑	☐
For irredeemable or undated bonds, the higher the issue price the higher the yield for the investor who subscribes for them.	☐	☑
Zero coupon bonds must be redeemed at par in order to give the lender an appropriate yield to maturity.	☐	☑

By definition deep discounted bonds (DDB) will have a lower market price than nominal value and sometimes the coupon rate will be lower than that of other bonds of similar risk. Both of these features generally mean that the DDB has to be redeemed at a premium when the redemption date arrives.

Bonds that have high issue prices will have low yields because the interest and the redemption value will be relatively small compared to the investor's outlay.

Zero coupon bonds usually have to be redeemed at a premium in order to generate a sufficient overall return for the lender so they do not have to be redeemed at par as the statement suggests.

3.9   The correct answers are:

- **The issue costs are likely to be lower.**
- **The regulatory requirements will be less onerous.**
- **The funds can be raised more quickly.**

Explanation

The issue costs are likely to be lower. This is true as it will avoid the high costs associated with issuing debt to public investors using the capital markets.

The regulatory requirements will be less onerous. This is true as it avoids the onerous reporting and regulatory requirements that come with issuing publically traded bonds.

The funds can be raised more quickly. This is true as it is direct arrangement with institutional investors and avoids the time-consuming process of issuing bonds on the capital markets.

Incorrect answers:

The coupon rate is likely to be lower – no, the coupon rate is likely to be higher due to the decreased liquidity of the bonds.

A larger amount of finance can be raised – a smaller amount of finance is normally raised from a private placement due to the reduced number of investors.

3.10   The correct answer is: **$2.50.**

The minimum share price at which an investor would opt to convert is $2.40, since this is the price at which the value of the shares received would match the cash received on redemption ($120 / 50 = $2.40).

$2.50 is above this price and therefore the bonds would be converted rather than redeemed.

3.11   The correct answer is: **Financial statements of Xyrox Co for the last three years.**

Future performance will be critical to bank's analysis, and anyway the financial statements will not come as a surprise to Xyrox's bank which will be aware of these anyway.

3.12 The correct answer is: **Convertible bonds have a lower coupon rate.**

Convertible bonds are not treated as equity, they are still a financial liability and will increase the gearing ratio.

Convertible bonds are likely to have a higher yield to maturity due to the possibility that they are converted into to equity capital which is more expensive.

Convertible bonds do have a redemption cost. There is no cash flow on conversion but there is still a cost attached to converting the bonds into ordinary shares.

3.13 The correct answer is: **$31,700**

Cash flows are discounted at the after-tax cost of borrowing of 9%.

Year	Item	Cash flow	Discount factor 9%	PV
0	Equipment cost	(50,000)	1.000	(50,000)
5	Post-tax trade-in value (10,000 × 0.7)	7,000	0.650	4,550
1	Tax savings from allowances (30% × $50,000)	15,000	0.917	13,755
				(31,695)

3.14 The correct answer is: **$33,832**

Cash flows are discounted at the after-tax cost of borrowing = 12.9% × 70% = 9.03%, say 9%.

Year	Lease payment	Tax savings	Discount factor 9%	PV
1–5	(12,000)		3.890	(46,680)
2–6		3,600	3.569	12,848
				(33,832)

Six-year cumulative present value factor = 4.486

One-year present value factor = (0.917)

3.569

3.15 The correct answer is: **The post-tax cost of HiFli's proposed loan.**

The analysis of **whether or not to make the acquisition** should be based on a risk-adjusted cost of capital.

However, once the decision has been made to complete the acquisition the issue is **whether the lease is more or less expensive than the bank loan.**

For this reason the cost of the bank loan becomes the appropriate cost of capital, and the cost of the bank loan should be adjusted for the impact of tax (by multiplying by (1 – t)) to reflect its true cost to HiFli.

3.16 The correct answers are:

- **It is incorrect to include the interest on the loan in the buy option.**
- **The timing of the lease payments are incorrect.**
- **Using a discount rate of 5% is incorrect.**

Explanation

It is incorrect to include the interest on the loan in the buy option – the interest on the loan should not be included as this is incorporated via the discount factor.

The timing of the lease payments are incorrect – the lease is payable in advance and therefore the lease payments should be in T0 – 3.

Using a discount rate of 5% is incorrect – the discount factor should be the post-tax cost of borrowing and therefore should be 5% (1 – 0.2) = 4%.

Incorrect answers:

The tax allowable depreciation calculation in the buy option is incorrect. No, the calculations are correct based on straight line.

The timing of the tax relief on the lease payments is incorrect. No, the timing is correct, The first lease payment would be on 1 January 20X1 (T0) with the tax relief available at the end of that year (31 December 20X1) which is time period 1.

4 Equity finance

4.1 The correct answer is: **$7,500 million**

Price $	Millions of shares applied for at this price	Cumulative applications
3.00	50	50
2.90	100	~~100~~ 150
2.80	250	400
2.70	500	900
2.60	1,000	1,900
2.50	1,700	3,600

Cumulative applications, working downwards in prices tendered, reach 3,000 million at a price of $2.50.

The issue price will therefore be $2.50 and $7,500 million ($2.5 × 3,000 million) will be raised.

4.2 The correct answer is: **8%**

K_e $= r_f + (r_m - r_f)$ beta
9         $= 3 + (r_m - 3)1.2$
6         $= 1.2r_m - 3 \times 1.2$
6 + 3.6 $= 1.2r_m$ so $r_m = 9.6 / 1.2 = 8$

4.3 The correct answers are:

Gearing (debt/debt + equity)	Decrease
Share premium account	Increase

A rights issue will increase the proportion of the capital structure that consists of equity, so gearing will fall.

The share premium account will rise because the issue price of $3 × 0.6 = $1.80 is above the nominal value per share so the share premium account will rise by the excess ($0.80 per share).

4.4 The correct answer is: **23%.**

Dividend per share, 20X5	=	$379,000/2 million
	=	18.95c
The dividend growth in four years 20X1-20X5 has been	=	379,000/300,000
	=	1.2633
Fourth root of 1.2633	=	0.06 approx, or 6% per annum
$K_e = d_1/P_0 + g$	=	$(0.1895 \times 1.06)/1.18 + 0.06 = 0.23$ or 23%

It is easy to misread the question and to think that growth is over five years because there are five rows of data, but a moment's thought should clarify that there are four years between 20X1 and 20X5.

If you used earnings growth then you would obtain a 4% growth rate and a cost of equity of 21%. However, where you are given dividend growth then this should be used in the dividend growth model.

4.5 The correct answer is: **The risk that can be eliminated by diversification.**

This is the risk that is specific to a company.

Systematic or market risk **cannot** be eliminated by diversification.

4.6 The correct answers are:

	True	False
The capital asset pricing model can be used to calculate the cost of equity of an entity. Unlike the dividend growth model, CAPM specifically factors risk into the calculation.	☑	☐
The Beta factor is a measure of the total risk associated with a share or security.	☐	☑

CAPM factors risk into the calculation of the cost of equity by including a beta factor in its formula.

Beta factors measure the systematic risk of a security but not the specific, unsystematic risk.

4.7 The correct answer is: **Worse off.**

If shareholders sell their rights at $0.2 per share held then the holder of 10 shares will receive $2 (0.2 × 10), and their wealth after the rights issue will be $57 (10 shares worth $55 + $2). This is **worse** than someone who takes up their rights.

After rights issue:

11 shares held × $5.5 = $60.5

1 share bought = (3)

Net wealth = $60.5 − $3 = $57.5

This is because the value being paid for the rights is less than their true value. The true value of a right is the difference between the value of the company after the rights issue (TERP = $5.50) and the issue price ($3).

This is $5.50 − $3 = $2.50

However, in order to hold a right, shareholders must hold 10 shares so the theoretical value of the right per share held is $2.50 / 10 = $0.25 per share held.

This price would compensate a shareholder for the $0.25 drop in value due to the rights issue.

A price of $0.20 being offered by B is therefore not an adequate price to offer for the rights.

BPP
LEARNING
MEDIA

4.8   The correct answer is: **$3.38**

The formula for a yield-adjusted TERP is:

$$\text{Yield-adjusted TERP} = \frac{1}{N+1}[(N \times \text{cum rights price}) + \text{Issue price} \times (Y_{new} / Y_{old}]$$

Applied here this gives:

1 / 5 [(4 × 3.50) + 2.25 × 9/7] = $3.38

4.9   The correct answer is: **C.**

Price offered $	Number of shares issued
$2.20	0
$2.30	0
$2.40	0
$2.50	50
$2.60	0

The highest price at which 50 million shares will be sold is $2.50, 69 million shares (44 million + 25 million) are demanded at this price. All applicants will pay the same price.

4.10   The correct answer is: **1.5**

Because Sonntag is ungeared its WACC is the same as its cost of equity.

K_e = $r_f + (r_m - r_f)\beta$
12   = 3 + (6)β
12 − 3 = 6β
9/6   = β = 1.5

This is an ungeared, or asset, beta because Sonntag is ungeared.

Note that if you mis-read the question and thought that the 6% was the market return (R_m) as opposed to the market premium for risk ($R_m - R_f$) then you would have calculated the answer as 3. This is an easy mistake to make – always double-check whether you have been given the market return or the market premium for risk before using the capital asset pricing model.

4.11   The correct answers are:

- **Cost of underwriting.**
- **EPS.**
- **TERP.**

The higher the discount offered the more shares will be in issue, which will affect EPS. The price after the rights issue (TERP, theoretical ex-rights price) will also be lower if the discount on the rights issue is higher becasue more shares have been issued at a lower price so this will dilute the TERP. Finally the underwriting costs will often be lower if the discount is higher because there is less risk of the new shares not being purchased by shareholders if they are perceived to be being offered at an attractive price.

Shareholder wealth is not affected by a steeper discount because althought the TERP will be lower if the discount is higher, shareholders have benefited from the ability to buy shares at a low price during the rights issue.

The WACC may well change due to the rights issue because the gearing of the company may well fall. However the amount of equity being injected is not affected by the level of discount being offered, so the discount is unlikely to affect the WACC.

4.12   The correct answer is: **Risk-free rate of return with an additional premium for systematic risk.**

$K_e = R_f + (R_m - R_f)\beta$

The premium is calculated by multiplying the beta (which measures systematic risk) by the difference between the average market rate of return and the risk-free rate of return.

4.13   The correct answer is: **5.3%.**

	20X1	20X2	20X3	20X4
EPS	1.2	1.067	1.2	1.4

$$\sqrt[n]{\text{latest EPS} / \text{earliest EPS}} - 1$$

$\sqrt[n]{1.4/1.2} - 1 = 0.053$ or 5.3% (where $n = 3$)

If you used four years you get 3.9%. However, there are only three years **between** 20X1 and 20X4.

If you used total earnings you get the higher numbers (20%+).

4.14   The correct answers are:

- Investing in a share that has a high standard deviation can reduce systematic risk in the investor's portfolio.
- Unsystematic risk refers to the variability of returns from a share due to factors unique to the firm's context
- Unsystematic risk can only be reduced by investing in a diversified portfolio of investments

A high standard deviation means that the total risk (systematic and unsystematic) is high. If the correlation between the new share and the rest of the portfolio is low or negative then the unsystematic risk can be diversified away leaving the systematic risk. If the systematic risk of the new share is low then the portfolio may experience a reduction in its systematic risk overall.

By definition unsystematic risk refers to the variability of returns due to factors that are specific or unique to the firm's context.

Standard deviation is used to measure total risk or variability (not the systematic risk).

Systematic risk cannot be reduced simply by investing in a diversified portfolio.

Including one extra share in a portfolio may not always lead to a reduction in unsystematic risk. It depends on the extent of the diversification already in place and the correlation the new share has with the rest of the portfolio.

4.15   The correct answer is: **$70m.**

Using $g = r \times b$

if $g = 0.03$ and $r = 0.1$ then

$0.03 = 0.1 \times b$

so $b = 0.03 / 0.1 = 0.3$ or 30%

This is the proportion of earnings reinvested so the dividend will be 70% of **earnings** = 0.7 × $100m = $70m

4.16   The correct answer is: **$0.75.**

Using the formula to obtain the TERP:

$$\frac{1}{N+1}\left[(N \times \text{cum rights price}) + \text{issue price}\right]$$

Because this is a 2 for 5 issue, you need to restate this as 1 for 2.5 to use the formula. The issue price is $5.75 and the cum rights price is $6.80, so the formula yields the TERP as $6.50:

$$\frac{1}{2.5+1}\left[(2.5 \times 6.80) + 5.75\right]$$

Alternatively you can calculate the TERP as follows:

	$
Current value of five existing shares (× $6.80)	34.00
Issue price of two new shares (× $5.75)	11.50
Theoretical value of seven shares	45.50

Theoretical ex-rights price	= $45.50/7
	= $6.50
Value of a right	= $6.50 – $5.75
	= $0.75
Value of rights for two new shares	= 2 × $0.75
	= $1.50
Value of rights for each existing share	= $1.50/5
	= $0.30

Because this question asks for the value of a right, not the value of a right per existing share, the answer is $0.75.

4.17   The correct answer is: **The company's debt beta is: 0.30.**

Using:

$K = R_f + (R_m - R_f)\,\beta$

and applying this to the cost of debt

$4.2 = 3 + (4)\,\beta$

$1.2 / 4 = \beta$

$\beta = 0.30$

Remember that the equity risk premium is $(R_m - R_f)$, and is not the same thing as the market return (if you used 4% as the market return you get the answer to be 1.2).

If you got the answer to be 0.09 then you used the post tax cost of debt, but the CAPM delivers the anticipated **pre-tax** cost of debt.

4.18   The correct answer is: **2.8**

$$\text{Yield adjusted TERP} = \frac{1}{N+1}[(N \times \text{cum-rights price}) + \text{Issue price} \times (Y_{new} / Y_{old}]$$

Here the issue price is $2.80 \times 0.75 = 2.1$, so the formula yields the answer as 2.80:

$$\frac{1}{5+1}[(5 \times 2.80) + 2.10 \times (16/12)]$$

The reason for this is that the extra yield from the project exactly compensates for the impact of issuing new shares at a discount to the current market price.

5   Dividend policy

5.1   The correct answer is: **Defer the interim dividend.**

Action needs to be taken to prevent the overdraft limit being breached.

The taxation payment should not be deferred because the tax authority can charge interest and fine the company.

Cancelling the widely anticipated interim dividend will not be favoured by the shareholders but would bring the overdraft down to within the limit in May and June.

The capital expenditure should not be deferred because the machine will generate future positive cash flows and net present value.

The company therefore may be in a position to pay an enhanced final dividend at the end of the year, so the interim dividend should be deferred.

5.2   The correct answers are:

- **For a bank wishing to increase its capital adequacy ratios.**
- **To retain cash to finance investment.**

A bank wishing to increase its capital adequacy ratios is likely to be doing this to meet regulatory targets and to reassure shareholders – it is unlikely that shareholders would want this to be compromised for the sake of a cash dividend.

Retaining cash to finance investment would potentially create more value for shareholders than they would receive from a cash dividend – this would be the case if the projects deliver a positive NPV. This would be preferable to a cash dividend.

A company wish to fund a share buyback programme may well decide not to pay a cash dividend. However, it is difficult to see the logic of buying back shares and then giving more shares to shareholders – so this does not seem to be a likely course of action.

There is no reward to shareholders from the payment of a scrip dividend because if more shares are in issue the share price will be diluted and this will offset the value of the extra (scrip) shares that have been issued.

Splitting the shares would make them more marketable by bringing down the share price – but a share split involves altering the nominal value of the shares so that more shares are in issue and this is different from a scrip issue.

5.3   The correct answer is: **Issued share capital will increase by $20,000; reserves will decrease by $20,000.**

Scrip issues involve the conversion of equity reserves into issued share capital at the nominal value of the shares.

A stock split involves no accounting entries because the nominal value of shares is unchanged, but this is not the case here.

BPP
LEARNING
MEDIA

5.4   The correct answer is: **Clientèle effect.**

The clientèle effect refers to the development of policies based on the expectations of the organisation's investors.

The signalling effect refers to the information content of a dividend as it is declared publically, which is irrelevant here.

There do not appear to be any restrictive covenants which are usually associated with debt or preference share capital.

The multiplier effect is not relevant here as it relates to a macroeconomic theory.

5.5   The correct answer is: **Constant payout ratio.**

The dividend is a constant 32% of the profits available for distribution.

A residual policy would mean dividends would only be paid after the capital expenditure requirement is satisfied.

A progressive policy would show an increase in the payout ratio.

Irrelevant is a term that relates to M&M theory without tax and does not apply here (tax is payable at 30%).

5.6   The correct answer is: **Residual.**

A company that wishes to grow in line with ambitious targets needs to retain its profits and reinvest them in positive NPV projects.

A constant payout ratio may also work but may lead to cash shortages, especially if it is unwilling to borrow significantly.

Stable growth in dividends are generally better suited to larger companies which are, in themselves, relatively stable.

A 100% payout policy is not feasible in the context of the company's growth targets.

5.7   The correct answer is: **Clientèle effect.**

The clientèle effect suggests that some types of shareholders are attracted to certain types of dividend policy. In keeping the dividend payout high the board is trying to satisfy their shareholders' need for large cash dividends.

The signalling effect suggests that the board is wishing to pass on information to the markets about the company's future prospects by setting the dividend at the level they chose.

Gearing and restrictive covenants are not relevant here as neither the capital structure or the requirements of current lenders are mentioned.

5.8   The correct answer is: **Shareholder return can be measured as the aggregate of dividends plus growth in share price.**

This is always true and therefore is consistent with the Modigliani and Miller (or any other) theory.

Whether steady growth, residual or low payout (high retention) – according to Modigliani and Miller it does not matter, ie it is irrelevant.

However, the share price **will** be affected by dividend policy because if the dividend payment is cut to invest in positive NPV projects, then the share price should in theory rise.

5.9   The correct answer is: **A small company listed on a small company stock exchange and owned by investors seeking maximum capital growth on their investment.**

This dividend policy will ensure that all investments are fully financed (an important issues for a small company). These investments should deliver capital growth on the assumption that the investments generate a positive NPV.

Where the tax on dividend is lower than the tax on capital gain, shareholders would normally place priority on the dividend payment – so they would not be happy to see the dividend being treated as a residue.

Where the company is unlisted and shareholders need to generate a return from their investment then they may prioritise the dividend because they are unwilling (due to the desire to maintain family control) or unable (since it is a private company) to 'manufacture' a dividend by selling a proportion of their shares.

A large publicly listed company could potentially use a residual policy (this has been used by budget airlines such as Ryanair in the past) but as a general rule listed companies are mainly owned by institutional shareholders who rely on dividend payments in order to finance their outgoings (eg pensions) – so they are unlikely to be happy with the dividend only being paid when there is a sufficient residue after necessary investments have been made.

5.10   The correct answers are:

- **A scrip dividend may lead to some shareholders receiving cash from the company.**
- **An enhanced scrip dividend involves offering shareholders a choice between cash and shares.**
- **A special dividend is the payment of cash to all the company's shareholders.**

A scrip dividend and an enhanced scrip dividend both involve offering the shareholders a choice between receiving shares and cash, but the share offer is more generous when it is an enhanced scrip dividend. A special dividend does involve paying cash in excess of normal dividends to all shareholders.

A share buyback will reduce the company's liquidity by distributing cash to its shareholders in return for some of their shares.

A stock split will leave shareholders with more shares rather than fewer.

5.11   The correct answers are:

- **Buying and selling shares bore no administrative or transaction cost.**
- **Taxes did not exist.**

Modigliani and Miller assumed no transaction costs and no taxes.

5.12   The correct answer is: **Finance from retained cash has no cost as a source of finance.**

Finance from retained cash does not incur transaction costs **but** has the same cost as the rest of the equity capital, because it represents funds that could have been paid back to ordinary shareholders as a dividend.

If the shareholders wish to make a **capital gain** then they will prefer their income in the form of capital growth rather than dividends. Thus they will be in favour of the company operating a policy of high retentions.

Since no change is made to the **structure of the ownership** of the business, the use of retentions does avoid the possibility of a change in control. This is a valid concern for shareholders in a listed company.

By using retained earnings to **fund investments**, the directors will not have to go to the general meeting to obtain permission for a further capital issue to finance new projects. It is debatable whether this is a valid motive, but it can be argued that the use of retained earnings allows the directors of Z greater autonomy in their decisions which may mean faster decision making.

5.13   The correct answer is: **An immediate boost to shareholder wealth as they receive funds from the repurchase.**

The **immediate value** of the company should in theory fall by the same amount that it has paid out via the share repurchase so shareholders should not gain or lose immediately as a result of the repurchase.

If a company has **surplus cash** then shareholders will, in the long term, expect a high return on these funds and if they are 'surplus' then a firm will not be able to deliver this. In this case then it is sensible to return the cash to shareholders to invest elsewhere.

A share repurchase will result in an **increase in EPS** and this may help to send a strong message about a company's financial health to the markets. Whether this actually results in a higher share price is debatable, but this seems likely to be a benefit at least some of the time.

An **increase in gearing** will not always result in a fall in the WACC, but sometimes it will and one of the reasons for this is the tax savings that will result from higher gearing. This is especially likely if debt is being used to fund the share repurchase scheme, which is often the case.

5.14   The correct answer is: **The company would become less able to respond promptly to new business opportunities.**

This would be the case because it would not have surplus cash immediately available to invest in such opportunities.

Vulnerability to a hostile takeover would be higher if the company **held** surplus cash because the bidder is able to use this cash to repay borrowing that they have taken out to finance the acquisition.

The special dividend would reduce the market capitalisation (the total value of the shares) by the amount of the payment but this is not the same as shareholder wealth; the shareholder would have the cash from the dividend to compensate for the drop in the value of the comapny – so their wealth would not be harmed.

Finally, the share price would be unlikely to rise because this has been signalled as a one-off and therefore will not affect the market's perceptions of the future cash flows that this company will generate.

5.15   The correct answer is: **$180**

Using $g = r \times b$

$g = 0.135$

$r = 0.18$

so if $g = r \times b$

$0.135 = 0.18 \times b$

$b = 0.135/0.18 = 0.75$

This is the balance of earnings that must be re-invested to generate the required growth. So 25% of earnings can be paid out as an ordinary dividend.

$0.25 \times$ earnings of $720,000 = $180,000

5.16 The correct answer is:

	Before the share repurchase	After the share repurchase
Cash (million)	2.0	0.5
Earnings per share($)	0.20	0.25

The cost of the share repurchase is 2 million × $0.75 = $1.5 million, so after the share repurchase the cash held will fall from $2 million to $2 million − $1.5 million = $0.5 million.

Before the share repurchase total earnings were $0.20 (EPS) × 10 million shares = $2,000,000. So after the share repurchase EPS will be $2,000,000 / 8,000,000 shares = $0.25 / share.

5.17 The correct answer is: **28.9%.**

There are currently 100 million shares ($50 million/$0.50). $15 million cash will buy back 10 million shares at current market value of $1.50 so there will be 90 million shares after the repurchase.

MV debt = $50 million/$100 × $110 = $55 million

MV equity = 90 million × $1.50 = $135 million

Gearing = 55/(135 + 55) = 28.9%

Incorrect answers:

26.8% – this is current gearing.

MV debt = $50 million/$100 × $110 = $55 million

MV equity = $50 million/$0.50 = 100 million shares × $1.50 = $150 million

Gearing = 55/(150 + 55) = 26.8%

Incorrectly starting with 50 million shares:

There will be 40 million shares after the repurchase

MV debt = $50m/$100 × $110 = $55 million

MV equity = 40 million × $1.50 = $60 million

Gearing = 55/(55 + 60) = 47.8%

Incorrectly using book values:

Debt = $50 million

Equity = $50 million − $15 million repurchase = $35 million

Gearing = 50/(50 + 35) = 58.8%

6 Capital structure

6.1 The correct answer is: **10.8%**

Using the M&M WACC formula:

$$WACC = K_{eu}\left[1-\left[\frac{V_d t}{V_e + V_d}\right]\right]$$

Where t = tax rate
= 0.25
V_d = 0.4
V_e = 0.6
WACC = 12 × (1 − (0.25 × 0.4/ 1))
= 10.8%

6.2   The correct answer is: **Parent company lends more to Anders Ltd than a commercial bank would.**

Thin capitalisation arises when a company's capital is made up of a much greater proportion of debt than equity. This type of capital structure is designed to minimise an entity's tax bill and is often used in overseas investments.

6.3   The correct answers are:

	High	Low
ABC Ltd was set up nine months ago and has ambitious growth targets over the next three years.	☐	☑
DEF Ltd operates in the high technology sector and has highly cyclical cash flows.	☐	☑
GHI Ltd operates in the service sector and has lots of intellectual capital but few tangible assets.	☐	☑

A new, growing business is at a risky stage of its lifecycle and it will be difficult to forecast cash flows with any degree of reliability so having high gearing is unwise.

Unstable cash flows resulting from a cyclical and dynamic business environment means that low levels of gearing are preferable.

A company with few tangible assets will find it difficult to offer security to its lenders so a low gearing ratio is preferable in order to avoid high interest charges.

6.4   The correct answers are:

- **The weighted average cost of capital of a company is determined purely by its gearing.**

- **The weighted average cost of capital can be minimised by using no debt.**

- **The weighted average cost of capital is irrelevant to a company's value.**

The WACC is the required return for a company's investors as a group. The factors that would affect that return would include many other things (eg business risk). However, the traditional theory of gearing suggests that all those other things being equal it would be possible for gearing to impact on the WACC.

If a company is zero geared (ie has no debt) the WACC will be the same as the cost of equity. The theory suggests that debt would be a lower cost source of finance so introducing at least a little debt would reduce the WACC. Therefore it is unlikely that zero debt would reduce WACC to its minimum.

The theory suggests that WACC is relevant to the value of the company because it is the discount rate used to find the NPV of the company's cash flows.

6.5   The correct answers are:

- **The company has no taxable profits so cannot benefit from the tax shield.**
- **Loan covenants on existing debt specify that debt should be lower.**
- **Interest rates are expected to increase significantly over the next three years.**

One of the benefits of using debt is the tax saving on interest payments. If companies cannot benefit from the tax saving then the attractiveness of using debt is diminished.

Loan covenants can be restrictive in this way. If covenants are breached then the borrowing company is in default and could have the funding withdrawn.

The company would not normally wish to INCREASE its weighted average cost of capital. Such a move would reduce the value of the company because the investors would require a higher return from the company.

If interest rates are expected to fall then the company would have no incentive to reduce its borrowings as it is about to become an even cheaper source of finance.

6.6 The correct answers are:

- **Modigliani and Miller's theory of gearing (with tax 1963)**
- **The traditional theory of gearing**

Both M&M's theory and the traditional theory suggests that the cost of equity will rise if debt is introduced into a company's capital structure.

The traditional theory suggests that WACC will fall as the company does so because debt is a cheaper source of finance than equity so the overall average cost of the capital structure will fall. Modigliani and Miller initially argued that the WACC will remain the same because the reduction in cost due to the cheaper debt will be offset by the increase from the cost of equity. However, when they revised their theory in 1963 they suggested that in a world with tax the tax savings on interest payments will bring the WACC down.

Trade-off theory and arbitrage did not specifically suggest a pattern of behaviour for an organisation's cost of capital.

6.7 The correct answer is: **Thin capitalisition rules.**

Thin capitalisation prevents a subsidiary reducing their tax bill restricting the amount of debt they can claim tax relief against.

High levels of political risk would encourage **high** levels of debt at WW so that it can minimise its exposure to local tax rises.

High levels of overseas corporation tax would also encourage **high** levels of debt at WW so that it can minimise its exposure to local taxes.

A forecast fall in the value of the Z$ would also encourage **high** levels of debt at WW so that BT can minimise its exposure to a fall in the value of WW's assets in Z$s.

6.8 The correct answers are:

	True	False
A rights issue is often preferred to a bank loan as a source of long-term funds because it prevents a reduction in earnings per share.	☐	☑
Operational gearing measures the degree to which a company uses debt to finance its operations	☐	☑
The ability to offer good quality security will usually reduce or maintain the interest rate offered by creditors	☑	☐

The use of a rights issue is likely to dilute EPS because of the issue of additional shares.

Operational gearing measures the degree to which a company's operating costs are fixed (rather than variable).

Security reduces the risk for the creditor associated with lending so will generally make the creditor happy with a lower interest rate.

6.9 The correct answers are:

- **Modigliani and Miller's theory with tax.**
- **The traditional theory of gearing.**

Both M&M with tax and the traditional theory of gearing suggest that WACC will fall as the level of debt is initially increased. M&M suggested that the WACC would continue to fall as the level of gearing is steadily increased but the traditional theory suggests that at an optimum point of gearing the WACC would start to rise again.

6.10   The correct answer is: **13.4%**

The cost of equity will rise as the gearing rises.

Using the M&M formula:

$$K_{eg} = K_{eu} + (K_{eu} - K_d)\frac{V_d(1-t)}{V_e}$$

This gives us:

K_{eg} = 11 + (11 − 5) × ½ × (1 − 0.2) = 13.4, ie 13.4%

6.11   The correct answer is: **Decrease.**

In general, the traditional theory suggests that the impact of higher gearing on the weighted average cost of capital (WACC) will depend on CER's existing gearing. CER's WACC will fall if CER's gearing is currently low, but will rise if CER's gearing is already at or above its optimal level.

However, if the company was initially **ungeared** (ie it had no debt in its capital structure) the introduction of debt will initially reduce the WACC as debt is cheaper than equity and any increase in the cost of equity will not be sufficient to increase the WACC.

6.12   The correct answer is: $9.93 = 11\left[1 - \left[\dfrac{39}{400}\right]\right]$

Using the M&M formula for the WACC:

$$WACC = K_{eu}\left[1 - \left[\frac{V_d t}{V_e + V_d}\right]\right]$$

K_{eu} = 11.0   t = 0.3 V_e = 300 now and so will become 270 after the buyback

V_d = 300 / 3 = 100 now and so will become 130 after the buyback

V_d × t = 130 × 0.3 = 39

V_e + V_d = 270 + 130 = 400

6.13   The correct answer is: **Gearing will be 40% and the bank covenant is not breached.**

V_e = 50 million × \$6 = \$300 million

V_d = \$150 million + \$50 million = \$200 million

Gearing = 200/(200 + 300) = 40%

67% incorrectly uses debt to equity based on market values 200/300 = 67%.

80% incorrectly uses the book value of equity 200/(200 + 50) = 80%.

33% incorrectly fails to add the \$50m new debt and calculates current gearing 150/(150 + 300) = 33%.

6.14   The correct answer is: **13.8%**

$$WACC = 15\left[1 - \left[\frac{10 \times 0.2}{10 + 15}\right]\right]$$

K_{eu} = 15%

V_d = \$10 million bank borrowings

V_e = 5 million shares × \$5 = \$25 million less \$10 million shares repurchased = \$15 million

6.15   The correct answer is: **18.2%**

K_{eu} = 15%

K_d = 7%

V_e = 2

V_d = 1

K_{eg} = 15 + (15 – 7) [(1 × (1 – 0.2)/2)] = 18.2%

7   Financial risk

7.1   The correct answer is: **To reduce or eliminate exposure to risk.**

7.2   The correct answers are:

- Company A is exposed to transaction risks. The currency received from Company B is likely to decline over time because of domestic inflationary pressures.

- Company B will be exposed to economic risk because it will almost certainly have to reflect the declining exchange rates in selling prices. This could make it difficult for Company B to make a profit.

Company A is exposed to currency fluctuations from trading the currency used by Company B but this is limited to transactions only – owning both assets and liabilities in Company B mean that a natural hedge in Company B's own currency removes any translation risk.

The inflationary pressures faced by Company B will affect its competitiveness in the long term, leading to economic risk. However, exporting to the country where Company A is based will not create a hedge as Company B pays Company A in its own currency.

7.3   The correct answer is: **Lower costs.**

Costs of using expatriates may well be higher including higher salaries, accommodation costs, benefits for expatriates' families (travel, school fees) and costs of training them about the country to which they are sent.

7.4   The correct answer is: **£116,500**

The daily volatility is required in GBP so USD 20 million is translated at the current rate of $2/£ to equal GBP 10 million.

Applying the 0.5% daily volatility value means that the one-day standard deviation = £50,000.

The VaR formula requires:

Mean + (standard deviation × Z score)

As the mean is not mentioned, we assume it is zero.

VaR = £50,000 × 2.33 = £116,500

7.5   The correct answer is: **Translation exposure.**

7.6   The correct answers are:

	Economic risk	Financial risk	Translation risk	Transaction risk
Company S	☐	☐	☐	☑
Company P	☑	☐	☐	☐
Company Q	☐	☑	☐	☐
Company R	☐	☐	☑	☐

Transaction risk is the risk that transactions are entered into at one rate and settled at another, usually due to timing differences. Company S is managing this risk using derivatives.

Economic risk is used to describe the long-term impact of changes in both economic activity and conditions upon the performance of a company. Company P has experienced the effects of economic risk due to currency fluctuations, interest rate changes and other macro-economic factors making its products less competitive than others in its industry.

Financial risk includes a number of different categories of risk, such as fraud risk, market risk and liquidity risk. In this case, Company Q has suffered from what it regards as excessive amounts of credit risk (the risk of customer default) and so is considering a solution to address this.

Translation risk is not related to cash flows because it explains the risk of assets and liabilities held overseas changing value over the course of a year when translated into the company's domestic currency at the end of that year. Company R has considered this risk and is looking to exploit it.

7.7   The correct answer is: **$164,500**

A$30 million translated at 1.5 = £20 million

The expected daily rate change is 0.5%

£20 million × 0.5% = £100,000

1 day VaR at 95% confidence interval = £100,000 × 1.645 = £164,500

7.8   The correct answer is: **Transaction risk.**

Transaction risk is the risk that a transaction in a foreign currency is recorded at one rate and then settled at a different rate.

Political risk is risk caused by government action.

Economic risk is caused by a medium- to long-term movement in exchange rate.

Translation risk is the risk that a company's assets and liabilities will change in value due to exchange rate movements.

7.9   The correct answers are:

- **It can minimise translation risk.**
- **It can minimise transaction risk.**
- **It can minimise political risk.**

Translation risk will be minimised as assets in B$ can be offset against a liability in B$.

Transaction risk can be minimised as interest costs will be made in B$ and can be offset against income in B$.

Political risk will be minimised as raising finance in Country B will help to maintain the interest of the local government in Country B in the success of the business. This could reduce the risk of harmful government intervention.

Simply having a foreign loan does not reduce the downside risk of interest rates increasing Value at risk measures the maximum loss possible due to normal market movements in a given period of time for a given level of probability and is not relevant here.

7.10 The correct answers are:

- **Economic risk.**
- **Transaction risk.**

Company A is exposed to both short-term (transaction) and long-term (economic) movements in the exchange rate.

There is no exposure to interest rate risk as Company A is wholly equity financed.

There is no exposure to translation risk as Company A is a single entity operating solely in Country A and will therefore not be exposed to a decline in the value of overseas investments.

There is no exposure to political risk as the governments in Countries A and B are stable.

8 Currency risk – exchange rates

8.1 The correct answer is: **Statement 2 only is correct.**

Even when a company does not export or import, it might be exposed to the threat of foreign competition in its domestic markets.

A strong domestic currency makes foreign imports relatively cheap. Borrowing in a foreign currency at a lower rate of interest is not a cheap option, because the foreign currency will be quoted forward at a premium, and its spot rate value could also strengthen over time.

Since the foreign currency loan has to be repaid at some time, and since interest payments will be made in the currency, the effective cost could be about the same as borrowing in domestic currency.

8.2 The correct answer is: **Invoicing in the overseas currency.**

Leading and lagging means advancing or delaying payments to a time when the exchange rate is favourable. Matching receipts and payments in the same currency reduces the need to convert currencies. Forward contracts hedge against changes in exchange rate and provide certainty in conversion. Invoicing in the overseas currency means that profits are held in the overseas currency. Remitting these profits to the UK will then be open to exchange risk.

8.3 The correct answer is: **Sterling will depreciate by about 6%.**

Applying purchasing power parity, the future spot rate in 12 months would be:

2.45 × (1 + 2% / 1 + 5%) = 2.45 × (1.02/1.05) = $2.38 per £

The annual change = (2.45 – 2.38) / 2.45 = 2.86

Over two years = 5.71% which is approximately 6%

If you stated that Sterling would appreciate, you misunderstood the erosion of inflation on Sterling – higher rates in the UK would mean that over time, its purchasing power would depreciate.

Of the remaining two options, 6% is closer than 3% so should have been selected.

8.4 The correct answer is: **£7,968,127.**

10,000,000/1.2550 = £7,968,127

As it's a British company receiving euros and the rate quoted is:

£1 = €X, divide by the rate quoted.

As the rate quoted is £1 = €X, the bank will buy € from the company at the higher rate, so that the company receives fewer £ for each € sold.

8.5 The correct answer is: **$1.4400 to £1.**

$1.52 × 1.08/1.14 = $1.4400

BPP
LEARNING
MEDIA

8.6 The correct answer is: **£1 = $1.6743**

Future exchange rate = 1.6500 × (1 + 0.035/1 + 0.02)

8.7 The correct answer is: **£4,321 profit.**

The Ruritanian $ buy rate is 3.4050

Sterling cost of imports = $130,000/3.4050 = £38,179

Profit = £42,500 − £38,179 = £4,321

8.8 The correct answer is: **Statement 1 true; Statement 2 false.**

Matching receipts and payments is another method of hedging transaction exposure, not translation exposure.

8.9 The correct answer is: **Receives £7,290,000; Pays £4,000,000.**

As we're looking from a UK perspective:

For the receipt as currency is quoted at €1 = £X we multiply by rate quoted, so receive 9,112,500 × 0.8 = £7,290,000.

For the payment, as currency is quoted at £1 = $X we divide by rate quoted, so pay 7,600,000/1.9 = £4,000,000.

8.10 The correct answer is: **The UK subsidiary pays $425,533 to the South African subsidiary and pays $56,322 to the Danish subsidiary.**

The first step is to convert the balances into US dollars as a common currency.

Debtor	Creditor	Amount in US dollars
UK	SA	R3,500,000/6 = $583,333
UK	DE	Kr1,400,000/5.8 = $241,379
DE	SA	R2,300,000/6 = $383,333
SA	UK	£240,000/0.7 = $342,857
SA	DE	Kr1,150,000/5.8 = $198,276

	Paying subsidiaries			
Receiving subsidiaries	UK	SA	DE	Total
	$	$	$	$
UK	–	342,857	–	342,857
SA	583,333	–	383,333	966,666
DE	241,379	198,276	–	439,655
Total payments	(824,712)	(541,133)	(383,333)	1,749,178
Total receipts	342,857	966,666	439,655	
Net receipt/(payment)	(481,855)	425,533	56,322	

9 Managing currency risk

9.1 The correct answer is: **€3 million.**

The payment will be $2.8 million multiplied by 1.0715, which is €3 million. The worst rate is always taken. For a payment this will be the higher amount of euros per dollar.

9.2 The correct answer is: **Unlimited.**

The worst possible scenario for a writer of a call is that the price of the underlying security increases to an infinitely large amount.

9.3   The correct answer is: **Sell euro futures or buy put options on euro futures.**

The US company will want to sell 1 million euros in two months, and could use futures or options on currency futures to hedge against the risk of a fall in the value of the euro against the dollar between now and then. It can do this by selling euro futures, which are contracts for the sale of euros in exchange for dollars, or it can buy put options on euro futures. (Each future is for 125,000 euros, which means that eight contracts or options would be needed to hedge the position.)

9.4   The correct answer is: **£206,540.**

Sterling amount = $300,000/(1.4545 – 0.0020) = £206,540

You always deduct a premium from the spot rate to calculate the forward rate.

9.5   The correct answer is: **48.**

The calculation is $2,800,000/0.938 (to get a euro figure) divided by 62,500 euro contracts. This gives 47.8 contracts. As you can't do part of a contract, round to the nearest contract, so enter into 48 contracts.

9.6   The correct answer is: **1.7805.**

Dollars are quoted forward at a discount, this should therefore be added to the spot rate which means that the forward bid and ask rates are 1.7805–1.7896.

The bank is selling dollars, and will want the more favourable rate, which is 1.7805. (At this rate, it will receive more in sterling for the dollars it sells than at the higher rate of 1.7896.)

9.7   The correct answer is: **$296,252.**

Forward premiums are deducted from the spot rate, which means that the forward rates are 6.7480–6.7510. The bank will be buying rands in exchange for dollars, and will apply the rate more favourable to itself, which is the rate that will cost it the lower amount of dollars. This is the 'ask' or 'offer' rate of 6.7510.

Your company will receive R2,000,000/6.7510 = $296,252.

9.8   The correct answer is: **$14,943**

Cost of forward contract	=	A$1,300,000/A$2.90
	=	$448,276
Minimum cost of currency if don't hedge	=	A$1,300,000/A$3.00
	=	$433,333
Maximum cost of hedging	=	$448,276 – $433,333
	=	$14,943

9.9   The correct answer is: **237.1   Let option lapse.**

The option premium makes foreign currency options quite expensive, and could therefore be unsuitable for any company trading on narrow profit margins. Options are often used by companies faced with:

1.   A currency exposure that might not arise at all; or
2.   Where the amount of the total receipt or payment is uncertain

Option premium	=	240 × 1.2%
	=	2.88 yen
Worst case	=	240 – 2.88
	=	237.12 yen

If the spot rate in six months' time is 245, the company will allow the option to lapse, and buy yen at the spot rate; its all-in cost would be 245 – 2.88 option premium = 242.12 yen to $1.

BPP
LEARNING
MEDIA

9.10 The correct answer is: **€740,000**

As the current exchange rate is more favourable than the option price, Edted will allow the option to lapse and buy DKr at the spot rate. This will cost 5,550,000/7.5 = €740,000.

9.11 The correct answer is: **Additional funds will need to be deposited by the engineering company.**

9.12 The correct answers are:

Closing out a contract	The process used when completing a futures transaction
Basis risk	The underlying volatility that exists between the futures price and the spot rate of exchange used for hedging
Margin requirements	The minimum amount of money required by the exchange before a futures contract can be agreed

The underlying volatility of the spot exchange rate used for hedging may also affect the price on the futures market, but the term 'basis' refers to the gap between these two – 'basis risk' is therefore the volatility of the gap not the exchange rate (as this could stay fixed if the futures price and spot price move in the same way).

The minimum amount of profit required by the company to justify the hedge being used may be relevant in the decision taken by a company when deciding which hedging technique to use but the term 'margin' refers to the minimum amount of money that must be retained in a company's account at the exchange before the contract can be honoured.

'Closing out' a contract is the term used to describe the process of completing a futures transaction – it may require certain controls but they are irrelevant to this definition.

9.13 The correct answer is: **A gain of US$6,250.**

When calculating the outcome of the futures transaction (assuming it has been set up correctly), if a loss has been suffered on the spot market, a gain must have been made on the futures market.

To select the correct currency denomination you need to remember that the tick value is calculated as $0.0001 per £ (the smallest movement in the value of the Sterling contract due to variation in the exchange rate). This is calculated as $0.0001 × £62,500 = $6.25 per tick (note that this is in US$ as the value of £62,500 is always the same in £ regardless of the US$ exchange rate, but buying or selling £ is more or less expensive to someone who trades in US$ as the exchange rate fluctuates).

Therefore, the total gain = $6.25 × 100 ticks × 10 contracts = $6,250.

Note. You were not asked to calculate the gain here but that may happen in the real OT exam so remember the number of contracts used as well as the gain or loss on each one.

9.14 The correct answer is: **£ put options.**

The options are denominated in £ so US$ options are obviously incorrect. The challenge is whether to select put or call options. The US company wishes to sell the £ it receives from its UK customer because it trades in US$ and the contracts are denominated in £, so will wish to acquire contracts that allow it an option (the right but not the obligation) to sell £. The option to sell is a put option.

9.15 The correct answer is: **$167,999.**

Money market hedge

Expected receipt after three months = 300,000 euros

Borrowing cost in Europe for three months is not given in annual terms and so does not need to be adjusted = 1.35%

Euros to borrow now in order to have 300,000 liability after three months = 300,000/1.0135 = 296,004 euros.

Spot rate for selling euros = 1.7822 per $1

Dollar deposit from borrowed euros at spot = 296,004/1.7822 = $166,089

Country C interest rate over three months = 1.15%

Value in three months of deposit = $166,089 × 1.0115 = $167,999

9.16 The correct answer is: **$7,122,195.**

The US company should borrow US$ immediately and send it to Europe. It should be left on deposit in € for three months then used to pay the supplier.

The amount to put on deposit today = €3.5m × 1/(1 + (0.01/4)) = €3,491,272.

This will cost €3,491,272 × $2 = $6,982,544 today (note $2 is the worst rate for buying €).

Assuming this to be borrowed in US$, the liability in three months will be:

$6,982,544 × [1 + (0.08/4)] = $7,122,195

10 Managing interest rate risk

10.1 The correct answer is: **The risk to profits, cash flows or even a company's valuation from any change in interest rates.**

Interest rate risk arises for investors and lenders, as well as for borrowers, and risk can arise from a fall as well as a rise in interest rates, or from a change in the structure of interest rates.

10.2 The correct answer is: **Buying a cap and selling a floor.**

Buying a cap sets the maximum rate for borrowing. Selling a floor reduces the cost of the collar, but also sets a minimum effective rate.

10.3 The correct answers are:

- **Contracts are subject to basis risk.**
- **Contracts are only available for borrowing in a limited number of currencies.**

Basis risk and limited availability are recognised disadvantages of using interest rate futures.

Futures are available in set amounts of borrowing (eg £100,000 contracts) but these can be combined to hedge significant sums, so this is not a disadvantage.

Futures contracts can be closed out at any time before settlement date, so this option is incorrect.

10.4 The correct answer is: **6.05%.**

In the swap, the bank will receive the fixed rate and pay the floating rate. The higher fixed rate will therefore apply, 5.55%.

The company will receive LIBOR in the swap, and pay 5.55% fixed. It will also pay LIBOR + 0.5% on its loan. Its effective net payment is therefore 5.55% + 0.5% = 6.05%.

10.5 The correct answer is: **Sell a 3 v 7 FRA.**

To fix a rate for interest income, you should sell an FRA. An FRA for a four-month interest period starting at the end of month 3 is a 3 v 7 FRA.

10.6 The correct answer is: **0.50 intrinsic value and 0.16 time value.**

The option is in-the-money, because an investor could exercise the call to buy a future at 93.00 and sell the future at 93.50, a gain of 0.50. The intrinsic value of an option is the amount by which it is in-the-money. The intrinsic value is therefore 0.50, and the rest of the premium must be its time value.

10.7   The correct answer is: **If interest rates rise, the market price of interest rate futures will fall.**

If interest rates rise, the market price of bonds will fall, and so the price of interest rate futures based on these bonds will also fall. Call options on interest rate futures will increase in value and put options on interest rate futures will fall in value. The coupon rate of a bond is unaffected by rises or falls in general interest rates.

10.8   The correct answer is: **An interest rate future.**

FRAs and futures are both fixing instruments, while options and IRGs are insurance arrangements. A swap can fix cash-flows but is more concerned with changing the nature of borrowing between fixed and variable.

10.9   The correct answer is: **£1 = $1.4614.**

Using interest rate parity, the exchange rate in three months' time will be calculated as follows:

$1.44 \times [1 + (10\% / 4)] / [1 + (4\% / 4)]$

$1.44 \times (1.025 / 1.01) = \$1.4614$ per £

10.10   The correct answer is: **£61,000**

W will borrow £2 million and pay interest at 7%, but receive the difference between the FRA rate of 6.1% and the base rate of 7% back from the bank.

In practice, this will mean paying 6.1% per annum interest on £2 million for six months only.

£2 million @ 6.1% = £122,000 × 6/12 months = £61,000

10.11   The correct answer is: **6.6%.**

Without swapping, both parties borrow at a total of (6.8%) + (L+1.2%) = L+8.0%.

Swapping, they borrow instead at (L + 0.6%) + (7.0%) = L + 7.6% which is a saving of 0.4%.

Split 50:50 between both parties, Lucas Lodge saves 0.2% on its fixed rate of 6.8% = 6.6%.

If you calculated 6.4%, you added the differences of 0.6% and 0.2% to find the arbitrage benefits.

If you calculated 6.5%, you used the fixed rate of 6.8% less half the difference between the floating rates.

If you calculated 6.7%, you used the fixed rate of 6.8% less half the difference between the fixed rates.

10.12   The correct answer is: **Sell December short sterling futures.**

To hedge an exposure to a rise in short-term interest rates with futures, it is necessary to sell futures. December futures are more appropriate than September futures, since the December futures relate to a three-month interest period from December, whereas the September futures have expired and would therefore relate to a three-month period starting next September.

10.13   The correct answer is: **With the collar, the company has bought a series of consecutive interest rate put options at a strike price of 8% and sold a matching series of call options at 7%.**

A collar in effect is a series of matching put and call options. The company buys a series of put options, each with a strike rate of 8%, which fixes its maximum net borrowing cost at 8.50% (since the company borrows at LIBOR plus 0.50%). For each put option, the company sells a call option, which reduces the net premium payable. The call options set a floor of 7% to LIBOR, so that the net borrowing cost for the company will not fall below 7.50%.

10.14   The correct answers are:

- **The effective rate paid by Company X will be 5.0%.**
- **The FRA will result in a saving of 0.4%.**

The FRA allows Company X to borrow the LIBOR element of its rate at 4.7% which is then added to the variable element of 0.3% = 5.0%. When Company X needs to pay its interest, it will be charged LIBOR of 5.1% plus the 0.3% from its existing arrangement = 5.4% but the FRA will limit X's exposure to 5.0% which means that the savings made from this arrangement are 0.4% from the bank.

If you calculated the effective rate to be 4.9% you probably calculated the rate based on the lower FRA amount: remember that the bank will always 'win' so borrowing rates will always be the highest one quoted in the range, and the deposit rate will always be the lowest.

If you calculated the effective rate to be 4.7% you assumed that the company would pay the FRA rate only but it pays 0.3% above any rate arranged.

If you calculated the effective rate to be 4.6% you assumed that the company would pay the FRA rate only but it pays 0.3% above any rate arranged.

If you calculated that the FRA savings were 0.5% you probably calculated the gain based on the lower FRA amount of 4.6%.

10.15   The correct answers are:

- **Reduction of currency risk.**
- **Reduction of borrowing costs.**

Gearing would not be reduced by a cross-currency swap and default risk usually goes up because there are more financial obligations when swaps are used.

10.16   The correct answer is: **The bank will pay the company 0.35%.**

In the swap, the company will pay the fixed rate and receive the floating rate. For the interest period in question, the company will pay 5.65% and receive 6.0%, ie it will receive 0.35% net.

10.17   The correct answers are:

- **In the short-term rates are likely to be lower.**
- **Variable rate loans are easier to renegotiate.**

Fixed rate loans are normally more expensive than variable-rate loans because a fixed rate loan removes interest rate risk. They are also hard to renegotiate and carry heavy exit penalties.

10.18   The correct answers are:

	True	False
A currency swap can be used to manage currency risk and reduce borrowing costs.	✓	
A currency swap usually involves the swap of interest payment obligations between the counterparties but not the capital sums borrowed.		✓
A currency swap can reduce the borrowing costs of all counterparties as long as they wish to borrow in the currency in which they have a comparative advantage.		✓

A currency swap can be used to both manage currency risk and borrowing costs.

A currency swap is very similar to a vanilla interest rate swap except it is usual for the counterparties to also swap the principal sums borrowed and then to swap them back at an agreed exchange rate at the end of the instrument's term.

BPP
LEARNING
MEDIA

For a currency swap to generate cost savings it is important that the swap begins with the counterparties borrowing in the currency in which they have comparative advantage and then swap.

10.19   The correct answer is: **0.2%**

To be useful the swap must initially begin with Company S borrowing at a variable rate (their advantage in that market is 0.5% whereas their advantage is only 0.3% in the fixed market). This difference in advantage is 0.2%.

Alternatively:

	Company S	Company T	Total
With swap	L + 3	6.8	L + 9.8
Without swap	6.5	L + 3.5	L + 10
Saving			0.2

10.20   The correct answers are:

- Company A has absolute advantage in the debt market.
- Company A has comparative advantage in the variable rate market.
- A swap may be arranged to benefit both companies

Company A has absolute advantage in the debt market because it can borrow at lower interest rates in both the fixed- and variable-rate markets. It has comparative advantage in the variable-rate market because its advantage is greater in the variable rate market than what it enjoys in the fixed-rate market. As long as each counterparty has comparative advantage then it is possible to design a swap that will reduce interest rates for both companies.

11   Context of business valuations

11.1   The correct answers are:

- Greater presence at marketing events.

- Increased shelf space in supermarkets devoted to the merged entity's products due to better bargaining power.

- Access to new markets.

Sales synergies result in higher sales than those separately achieved by the pre-merger entities. If the merger can create a bigger brand awareness and greater access to distribution networks then this is known as sales synergy.

11.2   The correct answers are:

- To ensure healthy levels of competition and safeguarding the public interest.
- To prevent large mergers that create a firm with a market share of over 25%.
- To promote fair and ethical competitive behaviour.

Healthy levels of competition are generally seen to be in the public interest and this is therefore the main focus of most competition authorities; these bodies will often intervene to fine companies for uncompetitive behaviour or to prevent mergers that create large firms (eg market share > 25%) and in doing so reduce the level of competition in the industry.

This does not mean that large takeovers will never be allowed if this is felt to be in the public interest, eg greater efficiencies, higher quality.

The reach of competition authorities does not normally extend to controlling government policy.

Competiton authorities do not investigate all mergers and takeovers, only those that risk being anti-competitive.

11.3   The correct answer is: **Horizontal.**

The acquisition is of a company that operates in the same industry, at the same stage in the supply chain. It is irrelevant that the clientele is different.

11.4   The correct answers are:

	Horizontal	Vertical	Conglomerate
Being forced by the competition authorities to close down some of the stores owned by the acquired company	✓	☐	☐
Damage to the brand name because of lack of appropriate competences in the industry of the newly acquired company	☐	☐	✓
Being tied into using the in-house supplies provided by the newly acquired subsidiary	☐	✓	☐

If the acquisition is horizontal then the acquired company is doing the same kind of thing as the bidding company. This may create a dominant position in the market and the acquiring company may have to dispose of some of the stores in the new subsidiary.

If the acquiring company has no competences in the industry of the new subsidiary this suggests that it is a conglomerate acquisition.

Having acquired a former supplier the parent company may feel obliged to use it as a sole supplier rather than use competitor firms, even though this latter option may be more efficient or effective.

11.5   The correct answers are:

- Post-tax profits would be maximised if a low transfer price was charged for the goods and services mentioned.

- Anti-tax avoidance legislation in Country A is likely to impose a minimum transfer price.

Where there are cross-border transfer pricing arrangements it is better from a tax point of view to have profits in the country where tax rates are lower. In this case that means profits should be maximised in Country B. Therefore Company A should charge a low transfer price for what it sells to Company B.

If a low price is charged in Country A then the tax authorities there are likely to prefer to keep as much profit as possible in Country A so regulations would impose a minimum price.

11.6   The correct answers are:

	Conglomerate	Horizontal	Backward vertical	Forward vertical
A firm of estate agents acquiring a local construction company	✓	☐	☐	☐
An undertaker acquiring another undertaker in a different part of the same country	☐	✓	☐	☐
A supermarket acquiring a farm	☐	☐	✓	☐

Conglomerate acquisition refers to an acquisition of a company in a different line of business (despite there being a link).

Horizontal acquisition refers to an acquisition of a company in a similar line of business.

Backward vertical acquisition is the acquisition of a supplier.

BPP
LEARNING
MEDIA

11.7   The correct answer is: **This tax law will increase the attractiveness of Jordasian companies as takeover targets.**

The new law will mean that Jordasian companies (particularly those that have made losses) will become more attractive to foreign companies. However, the opposite does not seem to be true as the tax relief is only available to foreign parents rather than foreign subsidiaries.

The tax law will have no effect on the group's ability to conduct intra-group trade.

11.8   The correct answers are:

	Economies of scale	Synergies	Golden parachutes	Poison pills
The additional value generated from combining together two companies over and above that which would be generated if the companies were kept separate	☐	☑	☐	☐
Large severance pay deals for directors triggered by a serious takeover bid by a third party	☐	☐	☑	☐
Savings in cost that are generated by an entity becoming larger	☑	☐	☐	☐

11.9   The correct answer is: **$15 million.**

By paying $120m for a company that is worth $110m before the bid and $110m + $25m = $135m after the bid – Company RS's shareholders will gain by $135 – $120m = $15m.

11.10   The correct answers are:

- Economies of scale.
- Reduction of competition.
- Increased market power.

Horizontal acquisition is the acquisition of a business in the same line of business. Therefore there are potential cost savings available from operating on a larger scale without significantly changing what the business does (economies of scale). The acquired company is likely, to some degree, to be a competitor so when it is acquired a degree of competition is eliminated.

Widening the business portfolio is the result of conglomerate acquisition. Acquisition of undervalued companies is associated primarily with conglomerate acquisition because it is less important what the acquisition target does than what its selling price is.

Securing key elements of the value chain is a potential benefit of vertical acquisition which involves the acquisition of a supplier or customer.

11.11   The correct answer is: **Horizontal.**

Competition authorities generally have the objective of preventing substantial lessening of competition. Although competition authorities around the world may have a number of reasons for investigating a proposed acquisition depending on the legal jurisdiction in which they operate, it is more likely that a horizontal acquisition will attract their interest first. This is because a horizontal acquisition involves one entity acquiring another in a similar line of business.

11.12   The correct answers are:

- **A's competitors**
- **The competition authorities**

Rivals are unlikely to be keen on being supplied by a company that is owned by a rival (A). This may mean that they make alternative supply arrangements – which in turn may affect the logic of buying B.

Customers in general are unlikely to be concerned by this; any concerns they may have over past mistreatment of staff should become irrelevant once A owns B and can change the way in which staff are managed.

A's shareholders will be concerned if the price paid for B is too high but this does not seem likely here.

Competition authorities are likely to be concerned, not because A is expanding its market share as a petrol retailer, but because of the market power it will exercise over its rivals as a result of this acquisition.

11.13   The correct answers are:

- **Plan to float the D shares on a stock exchange in four years.**
- **Sell the D shares in four years time to a private equity firm for cash.**
- **Arrange for the D directors to buy back the shares from S in the third and fourth years of the investment for cash.**

An exit route will allow the venture capitalist to withdraw from its investment and use its funds on other investment opportunities.

Granting an option to DKK to borrow funds from S9X will merely change the nature of S9X's investment from an equity investment to a debt investment. It will not be an exit route if S9X has to continue to fund DKK.

An equity ratchet is a mechanism which will protect the venture capitalist's investment in the event of returns being poor. This mechanism, however, increases the involvement of S9X as it will involve the transfer of shares to S9X or give S9X the right to appoint directors to the board. It does not provide an exit route.

A flotation will allow S9X to sell their shares on the open market. Arranging to sell the shares for cash will allow S9X to withdraw from their investment.

11.14   The correct answer is: **The acquisition of one company by another where previously one company was a customer of another.**

A vertical acquisition involves the takeover of one company by another where both companies are in the same supply chain but are at different stages of that chain.

Although many vertical acquisitions result in cost synergies, they do not define this type of acquisition.

11.15   The correct answers are:

- **Allocation of a greater pool of managers to projects in order to optimise the use of their skills.**
- **Sharing best practice with regards technology.**

Management synergy refers to the improvement in performance that a combined entity can generate by managing processes better.

Sharing networks of distributors and retailers is an example of sales synergies.

More efficient use of tax losses and spreading risk over a broader range of products are financial synergies.

11.16   The correct answers are:

- **Cost savings due to economies of scale in purchasing.**
- **Reduction in staff costs due to elimination of duplicated administration roles.**
- **A reduction in the volatility of cash flows due the diversification of its activities.**

Diversification will result because Photon is moving into another, competing, sector of the market.

Sale and leaseback may be possible, but is less likely as a synergy because it could happen anyway, ie without the acquisition. So it is not extra value created by the acquisition (especially as sale and leaseback will involve costly lease repayments).

Due to the lack of direct rivalry between Photon and Ria, enhanced profit due to less rivalry is less likely.

11.17   The correct answer is: **Forward vertical.**

This acquisition is a forward vertical acquisition as the acquirer is at an earlier stage of the supply chain compared to the target.

11.18   The correct answer is: **An acquisition of Office Direct Co, a firm that operates in the same region supplying luxury office refurbishments.**

Venture capital would normally be appropriate for a business acquisition that would expand the business into new markets, thus requiring a significant injection of new capital and business advice.

Venture capital is also described as 'Risk Capital', as it is often used in circumstances where high risk and therefore high returns are expected.

Neither the replacement of equipment nor the building would be typical of risky ventures because neither are risky ventures deigned to give high returns. The scale of the expansion of the design consultancy is probably too small to attract a venture capitalist.

11.19   The correct answers are:

- **Cost savings in production due to economies of scale**
- **Reduction in staff costs due to the removal of duplicated roles**
- **Enhanced profit due to reduced competition**

Cost savings in production due to economies of scale – this is a key synergy arising from a horizontal integration.

Reduction in staff costs due to the removal of duplicated roles – given both companies are manufacturers it is likely that there will be significant costs savings in duplicated roles such as administration.

Enhanced profit due to reduced competition – horizontal integrations increase market power and reduce competition.

Incorrect answers:

Cost savings in purchasing due to vertical integration – this is not a vertical integration, it is a horizontal integration.

Reduction in financial risk due to diversification – acquiring a company in the same industry does not lead to diversification.

11.20   The correct answer is: **Gearing will decrease.**

An increase in equity will decrease the gearing ratio.

EPS will decrease with a share issue.

There will be dilution of control with a share issue.

DPS will decrease with a share issue.

12 Introduction to valuation methods

12.1 Correct answer: **Semi-strong form.**

This is a definition of this form of stock-market efficiency.

12.2 The correct answers are:

Highest value:

Company 2

Company 3

Lowest value:

Company 1

Company 1 is worth $1200 million ($200 million earnings × P/E of 6)

Company 2 is worth $1600 million ($320 million × 5)

Company 3 is worth $1400 million ($400 million × 3.5)

12.3 The correct answer is: **250 cents**

KP's value will fall by $100 million as the cash is spent because this represents cash that could have been paid out as a dividend but it will then rise by the present value of the cash flows generated by the project.

$800 million − $100 million + $140 million = $840 million

This is an increase of $40 million on 16 million shares = $2.50 or 250 cents.

12.4 The correct answer is: **$360m**

Company X has 400 million shares in issue ($200 million / 0.5), so the total dividend is $0.10 × 400 million = $40 million. So after the dividend payment has been made Company X will be worth $400 million − $40 million = $360 million.

12.5 The correct answer is: **$2.06m.**

The minimum bid will match the sum that Naught Ltd could receive if it sold its assets and repaid its liabilities.

	$
Non-current assets	1,200,000
Inventory	1,160,000
Receivables, ($792,000 / 99%) × 98% = 784,000	784,000
Bank overdraft and trade payables	(1,080,000)
	2,064,000

If you chose $2.10 million you have neglected to adjust for the existing 1% provision within receivables for doubtful debts.

If you chose $3.18 million you have probably neglected to subtract the value of Naught's liabilities.

If you chose the net asset value (using book values) of Naught ($2.36 million) then you have ignored the information on realisable values.

12.6   The correct answer is: **A $0.24 drop in the share price and a $40m increase in total shareholder wealth.**

Currently AC's EPS = $0.6 ($120m / 200m) and therefore its P/E ratio = 10 ($6 / $0.6). So, after the rights issue the P/E will become 12 (10 × 1.2).

Currently shareholder wealth = 200m shares × $6 = $1,200m.

After the rights issue the new number of shares will be 200m + 50m extra (200m / 4) = 250m. Earnings will still (in the short term) be $120m but the value of the shares will have risen to $1,440m (120 × 12).

So the share price will become $1,440 / 250 = $5.76 which is a fall of $0.24 / share compared to its current level of $6.

However, shareholder wealth will increase because the company is worth an extra $240m ($1,440m vs $1,200m) and this increase will have come at a cost of only extra $200m of extra cash being invested by shareholders.

So there is an increase in shareholder wealth of $240m – $200m = $40m.

12.7   The correct answer is: **263 cents**

We can adapt the dividend valuation model.

$P_0 = D_1 / (K_e - g)$

Here this becomes

$P_3 = D_4 / (K_e - g)$

$P_3 = 0.4 / (0.15 - 0.05)$

$P_3 = 4.00$

Discounting back to a present value using a time 3 discount factor, this becomes 4.00 × 0.658 = $2.63 or 263 cents.

12.8   The correct answer is: **$14**

If 50% of earnings are retained and invested at 10%, annual growth in earnings and dividends should be (using g = r × b)	= 50% × 10%
	= 5%
Dividend next year should be	= 40 cents × 1.05
	= 42 cents

The share price should be, using the dividend valuation model:

$P_0 = d_1 / (K_e - g)$

$P_0 = 42$ cents $/ (0.08 - 0.05) = \$14$

12.9   The correct answer is: **Decrease.**

The financial risk of GER Co has risen.

Due to the nature of the investment, the growth prospects of GER are likely to remain unchanged.

Thinking of the share price in terms of $P_0 = D_1 / (K_e - g)$ this means that only K_e is changing, so the share price is likely to fall.

Eg if dividend is 50 cents and this is unchanged the share price would fall from 50c/0.14 (= $3.57) to 50c/0.15 (= $3.33)

There is not likely to be a change in the WACC (M&M no tax) but this does **not** mean that the share price will remain unchanged, as demonstrated above.

12.10   The correct answer is: **$11 million**

G's free cash flows = cash flows that are being generated for equity investors.

Here this is:

Profit before interest and tax adjusted for depreciation – interest paid – tax – investments in non-current and current assets

(note that the actual dividend payments being made are not included, the free cash flows shows the total amount of cash available to be made as payments to equity investors)

= (45 + 5) – 4 – 12 – 20 – 3 = $11 million

12.11   The correct answer is: **No efficiency at all.**

This investor believes that he can **beat** the market.

If all investors were acting like this investor then the market would actually be weak form efficient, but then the investor would **not** be able to beat the market.

12.12   The correct answer is: **$4.32m.**

A's P/E ratio should be applicable to B because the two firms are in the same industry, ie A should be able to 'turn around' B's performance (this is sometimes called bootstrapping).

So the P/E of A of 15× the earnings of B of $0.288m ($0.4m before tax – $0.112m tax, at 28%) = $4.32m. If you obtained $6m you have forgotten that earnings are profits after tax.

If you obtained $2.88m you have correctly applied the dividend valuation model but this model is not valid here because we can assume that under A's ownership B's value will rise.

If you obtained $4m you have incorrectly applied the dividend valuation model by using profits before tax as the dividend figure. As noted above this model is not valid here because we can assume that under A's ownership B's value will rise.

12.13   The correct answer is: **$4 per share**

As Company Z is a listed company the **minimum** value that Z's shareholders may accept is the current price that its shares are trading for, ie $1,000 million / 250 million = $4 per share.

Asset valuations are irrelevant to a listed company in this context, ie there is no point offering $3.2 / share ($800 / 250m) when the shares are trading at $4 / share.

12.14   The correct answer is: **$0.05 increase.**

The company value will go down by $10 million as the cash is spent and then rise by $15 million due to the market's reaction to the present value of the inflows. The net change will therefore be $5m, the NPV of the project. This is worth $5m / 100m shares = $0.05 per share.

No change would only be correct if the market was strong-form efficient and the inside knowledge of the project had already been incorporated into the share price.

$0.10 would be obtained if you divide $5m into 50m but the 50m is the nominal value of the shares in millions of $, not the number of shares (50c shares so $50m = 100m shares).

$0.15 is obtained if you forget to deduct the value of the outlay from the $15m present value of the inflows.

12.15   The correct answer is: **$34.61.**

A geometric average of the growth rate over the period 20X1–20X5 has been used, that is 1 + g = fourth root 0.92/0.65 = 1.091.

So g = 1.091 – 1 = 0.091

Using the dividend growth model:

$P_0 = d_1 / (K_e - g)$

Market value of share = 0.92 × 1.091/(0.12 – 0.091) = $34.61

If a five-year period is used to calculate the geometric average of the growth rate over the period 20X1–20X5 this delivers a growth rate of approximately 7.2% and a share price of approximately $20.55. This is incorrect because there are four years of growth over this period although the five rows make it look like there are five years.

If you forgot to apply the 9.1% growth rate to the dividend in the dividend valuation formula, you may have calculated the answer as $31.72.

12.16   The correct answers are: **CIV = [$80m – (11% × $60 million) × 0.65 / 0.10]**

Multiplying by 0.65 creates a post-tax value of the excess profits being earned.

Dividing by 0.1 converts this into a present value (assuming the excess profits exists into perpetuity).

12.17   The correct answer is: **$134m.**

Using the P/E valuation method requires two things: earnings and an appropriate P/E ratio.

Earnings are profits after interest and tax; operating profits are given here but operating profits are before interest and tax.

Interest = coupon rate × nominal value of debt = 0.06 × $18m = $1.08m.

So profits before tax = $22m – $1.08m = $20.92m.

So, profits after tax (earnings) = $20.92m × (1 – t) = 20.2 × 0.8 = **$16.74m.**

The most appropriate P/E ratio is 8 because this reflects the growth potential of this sector.

So value = P/E × earnings = 8 × 16.74 = $134m.

12.18   The correct answers are:

- **The valuation is understated as forecast future growth has been ignored beyond year 3.**

- **The valuation is understated as the directors have failed to include a perpetuity factor in the calculations.**

- **The approach used calculates the value of the total entity not the value of equity.**

Explanation

The valuation is understated as forecast future growth has been ignored beyond Year 3. Correct – expected future growth beyond Year 3 should be built into the calculations and will increase the valuation of Company B.

The valuation is understated as the directors have failed to include a perpetuity factor in the calculations.

Correct – Company B wold be expected to continue to operate into the foreseeable future and therefore a perpetuity factor should be built into the calculations.

The approach used calculates the value of the total entity not the value of equity.

Correct – the value of debt would need to be deducted to calculate the value of equity.

Incorrect answers:

The valuation is overstated as the directors have failed to deduct tax from the free cash flows. Incorrect – free cash flow to all investors is already net of tax.

Free cash flows to all investors should be discounted at 10% being the cost of equity and not 8% being WACC.

Incorrect – FCFs to all investors included both cash flows available to equity and debt investors and therefore should be discounted at WACC, not cost of equity.

12.19   The correct answers are:

- The industry average P/E ratio should not be used in these circumstances.
- The use of operating profit is incorrect.
- Current year profit is unlikely to reflect sustainable earnings.

Explanation

The industry average P/E ratio should not be used in these circumstances. Correct – a operates in a niche market with high growth and is unlikely to be reflective of the industry average. The use of operating profit is incorrect. Correct – profit for the year should be used. Current year profit is unlikely to reflect sustainable earnings. Correct – especially for a company experiencing unusually high growth in the last two years. The profit figure used in the valuation is therefore likely to be higher than expected future profits.

Incorrect answers:

The profit figure ignores the intangible value attached to A's employees. Incorrect – the extra profit demanded by the business (via its highly regarded tutors) will be reflected in the profit figure. It fails to take any account of expected future growth in the market. Incorrect – the PE ratio will take account of industry average expected growth, albeit this may be different from A's future growth.

12.20   The correct answer is: **$30.00 million.**

PBT $3 million

Expected based on industry ROA (10% × $15 million) $1.5 million

Excess return generated by Company B = $1.5 million

Less tax at 20% = $1.2 million

Discounted as a perpetuity at 8% ($1.2 × 1/0.08) = $15 million

Total value including CIV = $15 million + $15 million = $30 million

Incorrect answers:

$15 million is the value of CIV but not the value of Company X. To value Company X you need to add the CIV value to the value of tangible assets of $15 million.

$28.75 million is incorrectly discounting excess PBT as a perpetuity ($1.5 million × 1/0.08) = $18.75 million + $10 million = $28.75 million.

$18.75 million is incorrectly discounting excess PBT as a perpetuity ($1.5 million × 1/0.08) = $18.75 million and forgetting to add the $10 million tangible assets.

13   Advanced valuation methods

13.1   The correct answer is: **0.474 USD / GBP**

	Start year	PPP theory	Forecast end year
20X7	0.500	× 1.03/1.04	0.495
20X8	0.495	× 1.02/1.05	0.481
20X9	0.481	× 1.02/1.035	0.474

As the exchange rate is to the $, the $ is treated as the 'base' currency in the purchasing power parity theory formula.

If you obtained 0.527 $/£ then you have mistakenly used GBP as the 'base' currency.

13.2   The correct answer is: **Double tax agreement.**

Such an agreement aims to prevent the impact of tax laws which would otherwise lead to the same income being taxed in two or more countries.

13.3 The correct answers are:

- If prices are rising faster in Country C than in Country D the currency of Country C will weaken against that of Country D.

- If prices are rising slower in Country D than in Country E and in Country F, Country D's currency will strengthen against those of Countries E and F.

- Inflation in the UK is expected to be 2.5% and 3.3% in the USA. If today's exchange rate is $1.42 = £1 the expected exchange rate in one year is $1.4311 = £1.

If a country has high inflation relative to other countries its currency will weaken against the currencies of the other countries.

If the spot rate is $1.42 and inflation is 2.5% and 3.3% in the UK and USA respectively then the PPP would suggest that the exchange rate will move to 1.42 × 1.033/1.025 = 1.4311.

Here is the formula : $S_1 = S_0 \times \dfrac{\left[1 + r_{var}\right]}{\left[1 + r_{base}\right]}$

13.4 The correct answer is: **2.39**

This is calculated by taking the nominal interest rates in country Y and S, calculated using:

$(1 + r \text{ nominal}) = (1 + r \text{ real}) \times (1 + \text{inflation})$

so for Y = 1.02 × 1.03 = 1.0506 so r nominal = 5.06% (to two decimal places)

for S = 1.03 × 1.05 = 1.0815 so r nominal = 8.15% (to two decimal places)

IRP uses this approach: $F_0 = S_0 \times (1 + r_{var}) / (1 + r_{base})$

in this case the currency is quoted to the Y$ so this is the base currency, so the forecast is:

$F_0 = 2.32 \times 1.0815 / 1.0506 = 2.39$

13.5 The correct answer is: **When inflation rates in Country A are higher than in Country B, the currency of Country A will depreciate against that of Country B.**

The PPP theory examines the impact of inflation rates on currency rates. Where the inflation rates are higher it would be expected that the currency would depreciate.

13.6 The correct answers are:

A treaty between two governments whereby tax payable on profits made by an overseas subsidiary may be deductible against tax on the same profits in another country	Double taxation agreement
A local tax on remittances paid to an overseas investor – normally applied to interest and dividend payments	Withholding tax
A mechanism triggered by a serious takeover bid whereby the shares become more difficult to acquire	Poison pill

13.7 The correct answer is: **1.0146**

£1.05 × 1.032/1.068 = £1.0146

13.8   The correct answer is: **$140 million.**

FCF is the maximum dividend payable out of the current cash flows, and is sometimes referred to as **dividend capacity.**

This is calculated as:

Operating profit + depreciation – finance charges – capital expenditure – tax – repaid borrowings

400 + 140 – 30 – 180 – 90 – 100 = $140m

This is the theory that identical goods in different countries should cost the same. If the prices get out of sync then a change in exchange rate will ensue to bring the prices back in line.

13.9   The correct answer is: **Increase.**

The dollar will strengthen against the euro because of the relatively higher inflation rate in the Eurozone. As the cash flows of DUF are in dollars the value will increase as they are translated into euros.

13.10   The correct answer is: **Special dividend Z$7.65 million (G$5 million × 90% × 85% × 200%)**

G$5 million × 0.9 = G$4.5 million after withholding tax (note that corporation tax has already been paid)

G$4.5 million × 2 = Z$9m

Z$ 9m × 0.85 = Z$7.65m after 15% tax paid by Z.

13.11   The correct answers are:

Next year's expected dividend discounted as a perpetuity using the difference between cost of equity and anticipated growth as the discount rate	**Dividend valuation based on constant dividend growth**
Cash generated by the company after tax, reinvestment needs and debt related cash flows discounted at the cost of equity	**Cash flow to equity valuation**
Cash generated by the company after tax, and investment needs but before debt related cash flows discounted at the weighted average cost of capital less the value of debt	**Cash flow to all investors valuation**

A dividend valuation based on the assumption that dividends are constant would take the most recent dividend, and discount it as a perpetuity using the cost of equity as a discount rate.

13.12   The correct answer is: **Industry.**

The type of industry defines business the level of business risk and this is the building block for calculating a suitable cost of capital.

It is **not** essential that the proxy has the *same* financial structure because adjustments can be made to reflect the impact of the subsidiary having a different structure by adjusting the beta factor of the proxy to reflect differences in gearing.

It is **not** essential that the proxy is in the *same* country because adjustments can be made to reflect the impact of the subsidiary being in a country with a different rate of inflation to the proxy.

It is unlikely that the proxy will have the *same* size as the subsidiary. A similar size may be desirable but only very large differences in size would create a problem (on the assumption that small companies are riskier than larger companies).

13.13   The correct answer is: **X\$593m.**

Using interest rates to forecast exchange rates:

$$F_0 = S_0 \times \frac{[1 + r_{var}]}{[1 + r_{base}]}$$

The base currency is the Z\$, so in one year the forecast exchange rate is:

1.5400 × 1.02/1.04 = 1.5104

And then in two years' time this becomes

1.5104 × 1.02 / 1.04 = 1.4813

And the estimated receipt is Z\$400m × 1.4813 = X\$593m (approximately).

13.14   The correct answers are:

- **The calculations show company B's entity value, not its equity value.**
- **The valuation is understated as forecast future growth has been ignored beyond Year 3.**
- **The forecast exchange rates are incorrect as they show the B\$ strengthening and it should be weakening.**

Explanation

The calculations show company B's entity value, not its equity value. This is true. The value of debt needs to be deducted to calculate the equity value.

The valuation is understated as forecast future growth has been ignored beyond Year 3. This is true, the entity would be expected to continue beyond the three years included in the valuation.

The forecast exchange rates are incorrect as they show the B\$ strengthening and it should be weakening. This is true. The rate of inflation in Country B is higher than Country A and therefore the B\$ would be expected to weaken.

Incorrect answers:

The conversion into A\$ is incorrect as the assistant should have divided by the exchange rate and not multiplied. This is not true. It is correct to multiply as the value of the A\$ is less than the value of the B\$.

Cash flow to all investors should be discounted at 8% being the company's cost of equity and not 6% being WACC. This is not true. It is correct to discount cash flow to all investors at WACC.

13.15   The correct answer is: **Use the cost of equity of B, adjusted for gearing, as a proxy to derive the weighted average cost of capital for A and apply it to A's cash flow to all investors, then deduct the value of A's debt.**

Incorrect answers:

Use the cost of equity of B, adjusted for gearing, as a proxy to derive the weighted average cost of capital for A and apply it to A's cash flow to all investors. This is incorrect as it would calculate the entity value **not** the equity value.

Use the cost of equity of B, adjusted for gearing, as a proxy to derive the cost of equity for A and apply it to A's cash flow to all investors. This is incorrect as a cost of equity should **not** be used to discount cash flows to all investors. WACC should be used. It also fails to deduct the value of debt.

Use the cost of equity of B, adjusted for gearing, as a proxy to derive the cost of equity for A and apply it to A's cash flow to all investors, then deduct the value of A's debt. This is incorrect as a cost of equity should **not** be used to discount cash flows to all investors. WACC should be used.

13.16   The correct answer is: **15.2%**

Company A needs to create a beta factor using Company B's beta, but adjusted for differences in gearing.

$$\beta_{eu} = \beta_{eg} \left[\frac{V_e}{V_e + V_d[1-t]} \right] + \beta_d \left[\frac{V_d[1-t]}{V_e + V_d[1-t]} \right]$$

$$\beta_{eu} = 1.6 \left[\frac{(50m \times \$4)}{\$200m + \$50m\,[1-0.2]} \right] + 0$$

$$\beta_{eu} = 1.6 \left[\frac{\$200m}{\$240m} \right] = 1.333$$

This now needs to be adjusted using Company A's gearing:

$$\beta_{eg} = \beta_{eu} + [\beta_{eu} - \beta_d] \left[\frac{V_d[1-t]}{V_e} \right]$$

$$\beta_{eg} = 1.333 + [1.333] \left[\frac{50[1-0.2]}{100} \right]$$

$\beta_{eg} = 1.866$

$k\quad = R_f + [R_m - R_f]\,\beta$

$k\quad = 4 + [10 - 4]\,1.866 = 4 + 11.20 = \textbf{15.2\%}$

13.17   The correct answer is: **15.5%**

The asset beta is an ungeared beta; this needs to be adjusted using Company A's gearing:

$$\beta_{eg} = \beta_{eu} + [\beta_{eu} - \beta_d] \left[\frac{V_d[1-t]}{V_e} \right]$$

$$\beta_{eg} = 1.2 + [1.2 - 0.3] \left[\frac{1[1-0.2]}{3} \right]$$

$\beta_{eg} = 1.2 + 0.24 = 1.44$

$k\quad = R_f + [R_m - R_f]\,\beta$

$k\quad = 4 + [8]\,1.44 = 4 + 11.52 = \textbf{15.52}$

14   Pricing and post-transaction issues

14.1   The correct answer is: **The creation of a new company, where the shareholders of the original company own the shares.**

The offering of one new free share for every share currently held is a bonus share or scrip dividend. The sale of part of a company to a third party is a sell-off. The purchase of all or part of the company by its managers is a management buy-out.

14.2   The correct answers are:

- A high-growth company is acquiring a lower growth company in the same sector on the assumption that the acquiring company would be able to turn the target company's fortunes around.

- The acquisition of a company with a lower price–earnings ratio allows the acquiring company to create a higher EPS and share price for its shareholders.
- The post-acquisition value of the combined entity will be equal to the acquiring company's P/E ratio multiplied by the combined earnings of the two companies.

Bootstrapping in the acquisition of a target in the hope that the new parent company can impart some of its expertise and other strengths so that the acquired company's performance and value can grow.

14.3   The correct answer is: **The managers leading the MBO do not need to invest personally in order to obtain finance from venture capitalists.**

MBOs are disposals of businesses to the existing business managers, eg to the senior divisional managers. This usually ensures less resistance from senior members of staff while ensuring a higher degree of ownership among the managers. Because the newly founded company is likely to be a standalone company there is unlikely to be a dominant market position to worry about, so the competition authorities are less likely to investigate an MBO than a merger with an existing company.

However, before a venture capitalist considers injecting long-term capital into the MBO they will need assurance that the managers will also bear some personal risk.

14.4   The correct answer is: **Delay projects with an internal rate of return that is above Beta's cost of capital.**

If the IRR is above the cost of capital this means that the projects will deliver a positive NPV. The motive for delaying projects with a positive NPV is to artifically depress the value of Beta so that the MBO team can negotiate a lower price for the acquisition of Beta. This is unfair to Alpha Co's shareholders, ie it is unethical.

Employing more staff could have the same motive, ie to decrease profits in order to negotiate a better price. But for a rapidly expanding company like Beta Co it may well be the case that more sales staff are needed so in itself this does not look unethical.

Sale and leaseback would mean that profits of Beta would fall but that Beta would hold more cash so this would not necessarily allow the MBO team to negotiate a lower price for Beta.

Revaluing Beta's assets would be an essential part of the MBO process and is not unethical.

14.5   The correct answer is: **$25.67.**

New earnings = 1.25 × 15 + 3.5 × 2.5 = $27.5m

27.5/15 = EPS of $1.8333

1.8333 × P/E of 14 = $25.67

There will be 15 million shares in issues after the merger is complete (ie the original Co F shares as it is a cash offer – no new shares need to be issued).

Share price is $25.67.

14.6   The correct answer is: **30 million**

The offer for each S share will be $4 × 120% = $4.80.

Compared to Company H's share price this gives a ratio of 5.

Offer price per share	= 4.8
Total price	= 4.8 × 150 million = $720 million
No. of H shares required for $720 million/$24	= 30 million

30 million H shares for 150 million S shares

ie 1 H share required to buy five S shares or 0.2 H shares required to buy one S share.

14.7 The correct answers are:

- DEF's gearing will increase.

- The GHI shareholders may be taxed on any gain on the shares depending on what kind of shareholder they are.

- DEF's cost of equity will increase.

If shareholders are unwilling to invest any more in DEF then the cash bid is likely to be financed with debt so gearing is likely to go up.

Dilution of control and the issue of shares will only happen if there is a share for share exchange. There is unlikely to be any new shareholders so dilution will not happen.

14.8 The correct answer is: **Increase of $160 million.**

The synergies have a present value of $170 million. $10 million of this has been transferred to the Company T shareholders as a premium on the offer made by Company T. $160 million have been retained by Company P.

Combined value (450 + 150) = 600
PV synergies (17 × 1/0.1)   170
Cost of acquisition   (160)
Post acquisition value   610
Original value of P   450
Therefore gain   160

Other options either failed to discount the synergies into perpetuity or the premium offered by Company P was overlooked.

14.9 The correct answer is: **$84.5 million.**

Post-acquisition the number of shares will be 100 million + 2/7 × 210 million = 160 million.

With a target share price of $26.75 the market value of the merged entity will be 160m × $26.75 = $4,280.

Currently the two entities are worth (100m × $2 × 12) + (210m × 0.95 × 9) = $4,195.5.

Therefore synergies of $4,280 − $4195.5 = $84.5 million are required.

14.10 The correct answers are:

- To undertake an independent investigation into whether the acquisition has achieved its aims.

- To provide some organisational experience and learning so that future acquisitions are successfully executed.

- To give assurance that the synergy forecasts are realistic.

The incorrect answers are:

- To ensure the acquisition target's accounts present a true and fair view of its financial performance and position

- To ensure there are no hidden risks in connection with the acquisition

These objectives are the objectives of due diligence rather than post-audits. Post-audits should be undertaken after the acquisition has been completed whereas due diligence is done before acquisitions are completed.

14.11 The correct answer is: **$2,100 million.**

M&M suggested that a geared company is worth the same as an ungeared equivalent plus the value of the tax shield. $V_g = V_u + T_B$. This gives the value of the entity (debt plus equity) so the value of the debt should be stripped out this figure.

The value of the ungeared company (V_u) is 300/0.12 = $2,500 million.

BPP
LEARNING
MEDIA

The value of the tax shield (T_B) = 20% × $500 million = $100 million.

The value of the geared entity = $2,600 million deducting the value of debt gives the value of equity (2,600 – 500) = $2,100 million.

14.12   The correct answer is: **White knight strategy.**

Changing the articles of association and issuing convertible preference shares (an example of a poison pill strategy) are more likely to be used as a **pre-bid** defence strategy because they require shareholder approval.

The declaration of a special dividend is unlikely to succeed as it would probably be seen as an unimaginative one-off course of action – in effect a short-term bribe to retain shareholder loyalty.

A white knight strategy involves searching for a more acceptable alternative bidder and is often successfully used as a defence against a hostile takeover.

14.13   The correct answer is: **$95 million**

Value of the merged company	$195m
Value of synergy ($195 – 100 – 80)	$15m

Max payment for E Co = current value + synergy = 80 + 15 = $95m.

14.14   The correct answers are:

- **YY's earnings in $m.**
- **XX's P/E ratio.**

Bootstrapping involves the valuation of a target using the **bidder's** higher P/E ratio. It is applied to value under-performing companies in the same industry that a company feels it can turn around under its ownership.

In terms of the valuation of **YY** only YY's earnings and XX's P/E ratio will be used. If a post-acquisition value of XX was being calculated then XX's earnings would also be relevant but this is **not** the case here.

XX's cost of equity would be important for a cash-based valuation of YY but this is **not** being suggested here.

14.15   The correct answer is: **Increasing ED's EPS.**

A share-based bid (a paper bid) will dilute EPS when compared to a cash-based bid because a number of new shares will be issued. BN is a major acquisition as it is half of ED's size, so the increase in the number of shares will be significant.

The use of a cash bid will **not** dilute shareholder control because no new shares are issued. A cash bid will **increase** ED's gearing because surplus cash should be netted off against long-term debt in a gearing ratio calculation – so if this cash is being spent then gearing will rise.

Total dividends will fall if money is being borrowed as part of the cash-based bid, but dividend **per share** will still be healthier than would be the case under a share-based bid because no new shares are being issued.

14.16   The correct answer is: **$135 million**

$V_g = V_u + T_B$

$(100 + 50)$ million = $V_u + 0.3 × $50 million

V_u = $150 million – $15 million = $135 million

14.17 The correct answer is: **$5.625m.**

The latest P/E ratio for acquired logistics companies is the most suitable basis for valuing DP (as a premium for acquiring control will need to be paid).

DP's post-tax earnings are $750,000 × (1 – t) = $0.75m × 0.75 = $0.5625m.

Earnings × P/E = $0.5625m × 10 = **$5.625m**

Notes on incorrect answers:

$7.5m is obtained if the pre-tax profit figure is used – remember earnings are **post-tax!**

The other answers are calculated using the incorrect P/E ratios.

14.18 The correct answer is: **$4.33.**

Post-acquisition value = value of Fenton + value of Stork + value of synergies

Value of Fenton = 100m shares × $4 = $400m

Value of Stork = 40m shares × $2 = $80m

Value of synergies = $5m pre-tax × (1 – t) × 1/r = $5m × 0.8 × 1/0.1 = $40m

So post acquisition value = $400m + $80m + $40m = $520m

Post-acquisition no. of shares = Fenton's shares pre-acquisition + new shares issued to buy Stork Co

Fenton's shares pre-acquisition = 100m

New shares issued = 40m divided by 2 (1 for 2 offer) = 20m

So post-acquisition no. of shares = 100m + 20m = 120m

Post-acquisition share price is therefore $520m / 120m = $4.33

Note. The answer of $4.42 is obtained if the impact of tax on the value of synergies is ignored.

The other answers result from using the wrong number of shares (eg forgetting that Stork's original shares are cancelled after the acquisition).

14.19 The correct answers are:

- **Trade sale.**
- **Private equity buy-in.**
- **Management buyout (MBO).**

Explanation

Trade sale – selling to a third party would enable them to realise their cash investment.

Private equity buy-in – this would allow the directors to realise their investment. Private equity investors would be interested in the company with the hope of eventually cashing out via and IPO.

Management buyout (MBO) – the strong management team could buy Company A from the directors if they were able to secure sufficient finance.

Incorrect answers:

Earn-out arrangement – part of the purchase consideration will be deferred, payable upon reaching performance targets therefore this will not enable the directors to raise the full value of their investment immediately.

IPO – the company is not large enough to meet the listing rules therefore an IPO is not appropriate.

BPP
LEARNING
MEDIA

14.20   The correct answer is: **21.0**

Workings:

	Portas Co	Tribal Co	Synergy	Post–merger
Profit after tax	$200m	$80m	$45m	$325m
Number of shares	4000m	1000m new shares		5000m
EPS				325 / 5000 = $0.065 or 6.5c
Market price of shares	100c	250c		136.5c

Post-merger P/E = 136.5 / 6.5 = **21.0**

Practice mock questions

Questions

1. Summary financial information for Company A is given below, covering the last two years.

	20X1 $'000	20X2 $'000
Profit before interest and tax	8,700	9,500
Interest	1,200	1,000
Tax	2,400	2,800
Profit after interest and tax	5,100	5,700
Dividends payable on ordinary shares	2,000	2,200
Shareholders' funds	22,200	25,700
Number of shares in issue ('000)	9,000	9,000
P/E ratio	17.0	18.0

What is Company A's total shareholder return in 20X2?

○   17.7%

○   20.9%

○   12.2%

○   18.2%

---

2. Company A is a Company based in Country A with the A$ as its functional currency. It makes some sales to Country B denominated in B$.

The financial director of Company A is attempting to estimate the likely exchange rate in one year's time, so that he can assess the likely value of the entity's foreign income from Country B. Company A has a sales objective to generate A$10 million in revenue from sales to Country B in one year's time.

Sales to country B in one year's time are expected to be B$25 million. The spot rate of exchange is A$ 1 = B$ 2.5. Interest rates in Country B and Country A are expected to be 2% and 6% respectively next year.

What is the forecast spot rate in one year's time and will Company A achieve its sales objective?

○   Exchange rate: A$/B$ 2.41, sales objective met

○   Exchange rate: A$/B$ 2.41, sales objective not met

○   Exchange rate: A$/B$ 2.60, sales objective met

○   Exchange rate: A$/B$ 2.60, sales objective not met

---

3   Company A has set up a foreign subsidiary in country B, where the currency is the B$.

The following is an extract from the subsidiary's financial statements at 31 December 20X1:

	B$'000
Share capital (nominal value B$1)	100,000
Retained earnings	100,000
10% bonds	200,000

To minimise translation risk Company A has financed the subsidiary with high levels of foreign currency debt (in B$s) in the subsidiary's own financial statements. On 31 December 20X2 the tax authorities in country B implemented thin capitalisation rules based on the level of gearing of the subsidiary calculated as book value of debt to book value of equity. The required target is 85%.

Company A wants to avoid losing tax deductibility of interest due to a breach of the gearing limit.

The following information is relevant:

- The bonds were trading at B$110 per B$100 on 31 December 20X2.

- Operating profit of the subsidiary for the year ended 31 December 20X2 was B$60 million.

- Dividend pay-out ratio is 50%.

- Its P/E ratio is 10.

- Corporate income tax rate is 20%.

- No new bonds or shares were issued during 20X2.

Which of the following statements is correct as at 31 December 20X2?

O   Gearing is 68.75% and the thin capitalisation rules are breached.

O   Gearing is 68.75% and the thin capitalisation rules are not breached.

O   Gearing is 92.6% and the thin capitalisation rules are breached.

O   Gearing is 92.6% and the thin capitalisation rules are not breached.

---

4   **Which of the following is MOST likely to be an example of an 'economy' objective that a not for profit organisation might pursue?**

O   Minimising the cost per square metre of property rental costs.

O   Keeping total spending within budget levels.

O   Minimising the cost of dealing with a customer complaint.

O   Minimising the percentage of the budget being spent on administrative costs.

---

5   An all equity financed company has the following information relating to its most recent account period:

• Sales revenue $5.5 million
• Operating profit margin 15%

Due to difficult trading conditions expectations are that sales will decrease by 5% next year and the operating profit margin will fall to 12%.

Assuming all other variables remain the same, what is the likely percentage decrease in operating profit?

O   3%

O   20%

O   24%

O   5%

6   A company has the following information relating to each of its shares:

Share price last year	$2.50
Share price this year	$3.00
Dividend paid this year per share	$0.20

What is the annual return to investors?

[   ] % to the nearest whole percentage.

7   A company is funded by 5 million $1 equity shares and a $10 million bank borrowing carrying a fixed rate of interest of 10%.

The bank borrowing carries a covenant specifying the following two conditions:

• Interest cover limit of 2.5
• Debt/(cash flow from operations) limit of 3

The company currently has no other debt finance and the rate of corporate income tax is 20%.

The company is about to issue $5 million of 12% coupon bonds in order to fund a new project. The project is expected to increase annual operating profit by 20% from its current level of $4 million and annual cash flow from operations by 15% from its current level of $5 million.

The directors wish to assess the impact of the new financing and investment decisions on the bank covenants before commencing with the project.

What will be the impact on the bank covenants?

O   Interest cover covenant breached, debt/(cash flow from operations) covenant not breached

O   Interest cover covenant not breached, debt/(cash flow from operations) covenant breached

O   Interest cover covenant breached, debt/(cash flow from operations) covenant breached

O   Interest cover covenant not breached, debt/(cash flow from operations) covenant not breached

BPP
LEARNING
MEDIA

8   Vario Co is preparing an integrated report.

Match the following items to the MOST correct heading in the integrated report:

75% approval in staff engagement survey [▼]

Launch of a new brand [▼]

Cash in bank [▼]

Improvements in CO_2 emissions [▼]

Picklist:

Manufactured capital
Intellectual capital
Human capital
Natural capital
Financial capital
Social and relationship capital

---

9   Franco Co has a large cash surplus and is reviewing whether to use $2.5m of this to buy back ordinary shares at the current market price of $50.

Franco Co has 400,000 $1 shares in issue.

A trainee accountant has produced the following analysis of the impact of this policy on the wealth of a typical shareholder, owning 1,000 shares:

Wealth before share buyback =

(1,000 shares × $50 share price) = $50,000

Wealth after share buyback =

(875 shares × $57.143 share price) + (125 shares sold × $50 received per share) = $56,250

Which of the figures are incorrect in the above calculation?

○   Share price $57.143 after buyback

○   Share price $50 before buyback

○   875 shares, after buyback

○ $50 received per share

---

10   **Which TWO the following are likely to result from a company paying a scrip dividend instead of a cash dividend?**

☐   Lower EPS

☐   Higher market capitalisation

☐   A higher P/E ratio

☐   Higher gearing (calculated using book values)

11   P Co is a house-building company, its summary financial data over the past three years are shown below:

	20X1	20X2	20X3
Dividend ($000s)	500	547.5	599.5
Earnings ($000s)	10,000	10,950	11,990

What return on equity is implied by this pattern of earnings and dividends?

[   ] % to one decimal place.

---

12   Francis Co, a company whose gearing (measured by market values) is well below the industry average, has only paid a dividend in two years out of the past fifteen. Last year was one of these years.

Francis Co needs to raise finance to underpin its expansion plans, which are forecast to generate an IRR of 12%, and is considering the possibility of cutting its dividend in order free up the required cash.

Francis Co's current cost of equity is 15% and its WACC is 10%.

Which TWO of the following strategies would be MOST likely to be appropriate in this situation?

☐   Abandoning the expansion plan

☐   Raising funds through a rights issue

☐   Leaving the dividend unchanged

☐   Issuing a bond to raise the required finance

☐   Cutting the dividend to fund the investment

---

13   Wizz Co is a leading manufacturer of high-tech consumer communications devices. In the past it has paid out 20% of its earnings as profits and it has a ten-year track record of rapid earnings growth. Its share price is currently $500 per share.

Wizz Co is planning the launch of an exciting new range of products. This is expected to deliver an internal rate of return of 20%.

The plan has not yet been announced to the stock market.

In order to finance this investment, Wizz Co has concluded that it cannot afford to pay any dividend this year.

Wizz Co is also considering the introducing a 1 for 1 stock split.

Wizz Co has a beta of 1.8.

The risk-free rate is 4% and the equity market return is 10%.

Which of the following statements is MOST likely to be correct?

O   The proposed dividend policy is inconsistent with the objective of shareholder wealth maximisation.

O   Wizz Co's share price will be diluted as a result of the proposed stock split.

O   A stock split will increase Wizz Co's equity share capital.

O   A stock split will reduce Wizz Co's gearing (measured by book values).

BPP
LEARNING
MEDIA

14   Pedigree Co is a successful pet food company as shown by the following summary financial data for the past three years:

	20X7	20X6	20X5
Share price	6.00	4.00	2.00
Dividend cover	3.0	2.8	2.50
Earnings yield	5.0%	8.0%	10.0%

What has been the total growth in Pedigree Co's dividend per share between 20X5 and 20X7?

[   ] % to the nearest % (without including the % symbol).

---

15   VJ Co is a small ungeared vehicle maintenance company that is still 55% owned by the family of the founder of the company. The remaining shares are owned by a private equity company. VJ Co is unlisted.

VJ's current dividend policy has been described as 'progressive', ie dividends have been constantly rising.

VJ now has the opportunity to take on a large contract to maintain the vehicles of a national supermarket. This will require VJ Co to invest in extra facilities and equipment.

The finance for this could be raised by scrapping the proposed dividend for the latest year (which is about to be paid) and replacing this with a scrip dividend.

Which TWO of the following are problems with offering a scrip dividend in these circumstances?

☐   Pecking-order theory suggests that the founding family will continue to want cash dividends.

☐   The scrip dividend will create pressure on dividends per share in the future.

☐   Abandoning a cash dividend will send a negative signal affecting VJ's share price.

☐   The clientèle effect suggests the private equity company will be dissatisfied.

---

16   **In relation to Modigliani and Miller's theory with tax, which of the following statements is MOST likely to be true?**

O   Capital structure has no impact on the WACC or the value of the entity.

O   Increasing the gearing ratio will increase the WACC and decrease the value of the entity.

O   Increasing the gearing ratio will decrease the WACC and increase the value of the entity.

O   Increasing the gearing ratio will decrease the WACC and decrease the value of the entity.

---

17   Company A is an ungeared company with a cost of equity of 12% and is considering adjusting its gearing by taking out a loan at 6% and using it to buy back equity. After the buyback Company A's ratio of the market value of debt to the market value of equity will be 1:1. Corporation tax is 30%.

What is the new K_e for Company A after the buyback?

[   ] % to one decimal place.

---

18   Drilbit Co is a fast growing off-shore oil drilling company. It has just submitted an application to its bank for a substantial new 5 year loan to finance the development of a new oilfield.

Which of the following is likely to be LEAST important to the bank as part of its assessment of this loan?

O   Financial statements of Drilbit Co for the last three years

O   Detailed analysis of the possible environmental impact of the new oilfield

O   Estimates of the likely price of oil over the next five years

O   Expert reports on the value of the oil reserves that are being accessed

---

19   A Co is a large UK company with an excellent credit rating.

A Co is expanding its North American operations and, to finance this, is considering issuing Eurobonds denominated in US Dollars instead of conventional redeemable bonds denominated in Sterling.

Which of the following is MOST likely to be a motive for A Co deciding to issue Eurobonds instead of conventional redeemable bonds issues in Sterling?

O   Lower interest rates in the USA

O   To reduce its cost of capital

O   Eurobonds are often less expensive because they can only be issued by companies with a high credit rating

O   Eurobonds can be issued without granting security

---

20   Lenny Co has recently reviewed its debt portfolio and is concerned about its over-reliance on variable rate debt finance.

Lenny Co has approached a bank to discuss the possibility of an interest rate swap with a two year maturity on $5m of variable rate debt that is currently costing LIBOR + 1%.

The bank has quoted a swap rate of 4.15% against LIBOR.

If the swap is entered into, what will Lenny Co's resulting interest rate be on this debt?

O   4.15%

O   5.10%

O   4.10%

O   5.15%

21 Privet Co has evaluated a potential investment in the acquisition of some new photocopiers for its offices and has decided to proceed with the investment using its WACC of 10%. Privet Co is evaluating whether to acquire these outright or to use a lease.

A lease would require an up-front payment of $760,000 on 1 January 20X7 and four further lease payments of $760,000 on 1 January in the next four years. The lessor will be responsible for maintenance – saving Privet Co $208,000 per year.

Acquisition of the photocopiers would cost $2,000,000 and would be financed by a 8% bank loan. The acquisition would take place on 1 January 20X7 (the first date of Privet Co's financial year). Privet Co would be able to claim straight line capital allowances at a rate of 20%. After five years the photocopiers would have negligible realisable value.

The rate of corporate tax is 25%, paid the year after the cash flows generating the tax charge.

The full lease payment is allowable for tax purposes.

The lease versus buy decision has been analysed as follows:

Time	0	0–4	1–5	2–6
Costs				
Lease		(760,000)		
Savings				
Outlay saved	2,000,000			
Maintenance			208,000	
Tax				
Lost tax savings on maintenance				(52,000)
Lost tax savings from capital allowances				(100,000)
Net	2,000,000	(760,000)	208,000	(152,000)
Df 10%		1.000	4.170	3.791	3.446
PV	2,000,000	(3,169,200)	788,528	(523,792)
Net present value	**(904,464)**			

Which TWO parts of this analysis contains errors?

☐ The cost of capital

☐ The timing of the tax payments

☐ The tax calculation of 152,000

☐ The inclusion of the saved outlay

22 Sherlock Co has 5 million shares in issue trading at $5 ex div. A rights issue is planned at a 20% discount to this price to finance a new investment costing $4.5 million and the issue costs associated with the rights issue.

The rights issue will cost 10% of the funds raised.

Which of the following terms will allow Sherlock Co to raise sufficient funds to finance both the investment and the rights issue cost?

○ 1 for 5 at an issue price of $4.00

○ 1 for 4 at an issue price of $4.80

○ 1 for 4 at an issue price of $4.00

○ 1 for 5 at an issue price of $4.80

23 Company A is currently negotiating new fixed-rate finance and evaluating the following two options:

- Fixed-rate finance at 6%
- Floating-rate finance at LIBOR + 1%, together with an interest rate swap

A bank is quoting swap rates of 4.0%-4.5% against 12-month LIBOR

What is the impact on Company A's interest cost if it were to choose floating-rate finance plus interest rate swap rather than the fixed-rate finance?

O   Interest would be 1.5% higher

O   Interest would be 1.5% lower

O   Interest would be 0.5% higher

O   Interest would be 0.5% lower

24 M Co is a analysing the results of a tender offer which will result in it becoming a listed company. Currently M Co is 75% owned by its founder – Mr Croft.

Mr Croft does not want his ownership stake to be diluted below 50%, but aside from this wants to raise the maximum amount of finance from the tender offer.

M Co currently has 200 million shares in issue.

The tender offer gave investors the choice of four maximum prices. The results of the offer are shown below:

Tender price	Shares requested at each price
$1.40	100 million
$1.60	50 million
$1.80	30 million
$2.00	20 million

What tender price should be set?

O $1.40

O $1.60

O $1.80

O $2.00

25 Osgood Co is planning a rights issue to finance the investment in an exciting new project which is forecast to generate an IRR of 30% on an outlay of $8 million. New shares will be issued at a 36% discount to the current share price.

Osgood Co has 8 million shares in issue, trading at $5.

Osgood's WACC is 15%.

What is the yield-adjusted TERP?

$ [   ] to one decimal place.

26　Fenchurch Co is a publishing company planning a major investment which has been assessed as having a positive NPV.

Which TWO of the following factors would be likely to encourage Fenchurch Co to raise debt in preference to equity finance?

☐　If the investment is regarded as low risk and is expected to create reliable cash inflows

☐　If Fenchurch Co is a listed company

☐　If Fenchurch Co has a high earnings per share

☐　If interest cover at Fenchurch Co is already well above the industry norm

---

27　**Which of the following statements is consistent with M&M theory (without tax)?**

○　The cost of equity increases as gearing increases up to a certain level of gearing and then falls.

○　There is potentially more than one an optimal level of gearing.

○　The value of a corporate entity will rise as gearing rises but only up to the optimal level of gearing.

○　If taxes are zero then the WACC the value of an entity will be the same at any level of gearing.

28　A company has decided to lease an asset. The following information is relevant:

Lease payments	$12,000 payable at the start of each year
Lease term	6 years
Corporate income tax rate (payable in the year in which profits arise)	20%
Pre-tax cost of debt	5%

The full amount of the lease payment is deductible for tax purposes.

What is the present value of the leasing costs?

$ [＿＿＿＿＿＿] to the nearest $100.

29　G Co is an all equity financed company.

G Co has recently completed a review of its capital structure and as a result it is planning to introduce some debt into its capital structure by issuing a new irredeemable bond and buying back shares. This will result in a gearing ratio of 20% – where gearing is measured as the market value of debt divided by the market value of equity. Investors in bonds are currently expecting a yield of 4%.

The rate of corporate tax is 25%.

G Co currently has a cost of equity of 10%.

G Co's directors have estimated that G Co's cost of equity after the share buyback is as follows:

$$K_{eg} = 10 + \left[10 - 4\right]\left[\frac{20(1 - 0.25)}{80}\right] = 11.125\%$$

What is the error in this calculation?

- ○ The 4% should be adjusted to be a post-tax cost of debt.
- ○ Based on the numbers used, the Keg is not 11.125%
- ○ The wrong formula has been used.
- ○ The gearing used is incorrect.

---

30 D Co is an all equity financed company. D Co has recently completed a review of its capital structure and as a result it is planning to introduce some debt into its capital structure by issuing a new irredeemable bond and buying back shares. This will result in a gearing ratio of 20% – where gearing is measured as the market value of debt divided by the market value of equity.

Investors in bonds are currently expecting a yield of 5%.

The rate of corporate tax is 25%.

D Co currently has a cost of equity of 10%.

What will D Co's cost of equity be after the buyback?

- ○ 10.94%
- ○ 9.50%
- ○ 10.75%
- ○ 9.58%

---

31 Smart Co is a listed company operating a chain of coffee shops. As part of its expansion strategy it has identified Sunshine Co as a suitable acquisition target.

Sunshine Co is also an operator of coffee shops, but specialises in operating small shops at large transport hubs such as airports and rail stations, an area that Smart Co does not currently compete in.

Both companies are highly profitable.

The acquisition will be a cash bid financed by a bank loan.

Which THREE of the following factors are likely to occur as a result of the acquisition?

- ☐ Smart Co's beta is likely to rise.
- ☐ Synergies are likely.
- ☐ Smart's WACC is likely to rise.
- ☐ Smart's EPS will rise post-acquisition.
- ☐ Smart Co's cost of equity is likely to fall due to the reduced competition and therefore less risk in this sector.

32 Company A is an unlisted company specialising in the development of medical products. Recent results have been disappointing mainly due to its lack of finance resulting in it being unable to bring successful products to market.

To enable the company to raise new finance, the directors are considering accepting finance from a venture capitalist with the intention to float the company in ten years' time.

It is important to the founding directors that they retain a controlling stake in the company and they solely continue to make the key strategic decisions about the company's future. They are therefore keen that the venture capitalist does not provide solely equity finance but instead provides a mix of debt and equity.

Which THREE of the following are MOST likely to cause a problem for the directors?

☐ Venture capitalists will require an equity stake of at least 50% to ensure they have control of the company.

☐ Venture capitalists would expect a seat on the board and to be involved in key decisions.

☐ Venture capitalists provide only equity finance and would not provide a mix of debt and equity.

☐ Venture capitalists would normally expect an exit route within a period of less than 10 years.

☐ Venture capital finance is expensive and may prove too expensive for Company A to finance.

33 Echo Co is a listed company with a P/E ratio of 15.

It has 8 million shares in issue, trading at $3.00, and a long-term corporate bond with a coupon rate of 4% and a nominal value of $4 million. The bond is currently trading at $4.32 million and investors expect a return of 3.7% on bonds of this level of risk and maturity.

Echo Co also has 10 million 4% irredeemable preference shares in issue, with a nominal value of $1 and a market price of $1.50.

The rate of corporate tax is 20%.

What is Echo Co's profit before interest and tax?

O $2.56m

O $2.66m

O $2.40m

O $1.76m

34 Brighton Co is a listed company based in a developed economy with a stock market that has a reputation for being efficient.

A variety of estimates of the value of Brighton Co are provided below:

Market capitalisation	$219m
P/E valuation using an industry average P/E	$200m
Realisable value of assets	$125m

Based on this information, what is the MOST likely minimum valuation of this company?

$ [   ] million

35 Next year Aztech Co will pay a dividend of $12m out of earnings of $20m. Aztech intends to maintain this payout ratio in future years.

Aztech Co does not intend to borrow any money or issue new share capital in the foreseeable future.

Historically, Aztech has achieved a return of 15% on re-invested funds.

Aztech's cost of equity is 10%.

What is the value of Aztech Co's equity?

$ [   ] (give answer to the nearest million.)

36 Denhelm Co is a small unlisted manufacturer of high-quality organic pet-food. It has a well-established brand name and is looking for a stock-market listing to raise capital for further expansion and to reduce its gearing, which is above the industry average.

Currently Denhelm Co is profitable, and its dividends have been growing at 20% per year.

The average P/E ratio in the stock market is 15, and the average for pet-food manufacturers is 14.

The industry average cost of equity is 10%.

Which THREE of the following approaches to valuing Denhelm Co are MOST likely to be appropriate here?

☐   Use of a free cash flow to equity approach based on a cost of equity that is higher than 10% to reflect the need to compensate shareholders for Denhelm's higher than average risk

☐   Use of the dividend valuation model with the industry average cost of equity

☐   Use of the P/E ratio of 15

☐   Use of the P/E ratio of 14

☐   Use of the P/E ratio of less than 14 to reflect the impact of Denhelm's structure

☐   Use of a higher P/E than 14 to reflect the need to compensate shareholders for Denhelm's higher than average risk

37 Byfly Co is a low-cost airline which was set up over ten years ago. Some of its aircraft are leased, although most are owned.

Byfly Co uses a 'residual' dividend policy and has paid dividends twice in the last ten years.

In recent years ByFly has come under pressure to improve its customer service and has had some success in doing this. However, the cost of achieving this has resulted in it making losses in its latest financial year.

Which of the following methods would be MOST appropriate for valuing ByFly Co?

O   Valuing the tangible assets (using realisable values) and intangible assets (using CIV) of Byfly

O   The P/E method

O   Dividend valuation model

O   The earnings yield method

BPP
LEARNING
MEDIA

38 The founding directors of an unlisted geared company want to establish its value as they are intending to approach a venture capitalist for additional funding. The directors intend to sell 10% of the company to the venture capitalist. The funding will be used to invest in a major new project which has very high growth potential. They have prepared the following current valuation of the company using the divided valuation model:

$$\text{Value of equality} = \frac{\$50,000 \times 1.06}{0.10 - 0.06} = \$1,325,000$$

The following information is relevant:

- $50,000 is the most recent dividend paid.

- 6% is the average dividend growth over the last five years.

- 10% is an estimate of the company's cost of equity using the CAPM model with the industry average asset beta.

Which THREE of the following are weakness of the valuation method used in these circumstances?

☐ It is inaccurate to assume that the dividend growth rate will be constant.

☐ The dividend valuation model should only be used to value a controlling interest.

☐ The 6% average dividend growth rate is unlikely to be reflective of future dividend growth.

☐ CAPM cannot be used to estimate the cost of equity of an unlisted company.

☐ Using the industry average asset beta in CAPM is incorrect.

---

39 ZPP Co has paid the following dividends per share (DPS) in cents in recent years:

Year	20X4	20X5	20X6	20X7
dps	44.5	47.2	50.0	53.0

The dividend for 20X7 has just been paid and ZPP has a cost of equity of 11%.

Using this information, which of the following is the BEST estimate of the current ex-div value of a ZPP share (in cents)?

O 811.64

O 847.92

O 1060.00

O 1123.60

---

40 Company A has prepared a valuation of a competitor company, Company B. Company A is intending to acquire a controlling interest in the equity of Company B and therefore wants to value only the equity of Company B.

The directors of Company A have prepared the following valuation of Company B:

	Year 1	Year 2	Year 3 and each year thereafter
	$ million	$ million	$ million
Forecast free cash flow to all investors	10	15	17
Discount factor @ 8%	0.926	0.857	0.794
Present value	9.26	12.86	13.5

Value of equity = $9.26m + $12.86m + $13.5m = $35.62 million

The following information is relevant to Company B:

Tax rate	20%
Cost of equity	12%
WACC	8%
Debt finance	$10 million 7% undated bonds.

Which THREE of the following are weaknesses of the above valuation?

☐   The valuation is likely to be understated as forecast future growth has been ignored beyond Year 3.

☐   The valuation is overstated as the directors have failed to deduct tax from the free cash flows.

☐   The valuation is understated as the directors have failed to include a perpetuity factor in the calculations.

☐   Free cash flows to all investors should be discounted at 12% being the cost of equity and not 8% being WACC.

☐   The approach used calculates the value of the total entity not the value of equity.

---

41   Company A has the following information:

Number of shares	2 million
Shareholders required return	8%
Dividend just paid	$250,000

Dividends are expected to stay constant for two years, then grow at 3% per annum thereafter.

What is the estimated value of a share in Company A?

○ $2.27

○ $2.21

○ $2.58

○ $2.43

---

42   Company A is an online retailer of heath products. Profits have declined significantly over the last two years due to adverse reports in the press that the company has been selling illegal weight loss products. There have been reports that Company A may be facing liquidation due to the severity of the matter.

Company A's most recent statement of financial position is as follows:

	$'000
Assets	
Non-current assets	1,500
Current assets	250
Total assets	1,750
Equity and liabilities	
$1 Ordinary shares	500
Retained earnings	100
Non-current liabilities	800
Current liabilities	350
Total equity and liabilities	1,750

The non-current assets comprise specialised equipment with a net book value of $650,000. It is expected that the equipment would sell for $250,000 but would cost $1,200,000 to replace.

Included within current assets in a stock of inventory of the illegal weight loss product. It has a cost of $100,000 but would have a realisable value of zero.

What is the BEST estimate asset valuation of Company A based on realisable values?

○ $600,000

○ $100,000

○ $1,250,000

○ $250,000

---

43   Spearman Co has forecast the following cash flows to equity:

Time	1	2
$m	15.0	17.5

After time 2 the cash flows are expected to grow at 3% per year.

Spearman Co has a cost of equity of 11%, but is also partly debt financed with a corporate bond with a nominal value of $95m and a market value of $100m. Spearman Co has a WACC of 8%.

What is the value of Spearman Co's equity using a discounted cash flow approach?

○ $210.4m

○ $252.7m

○ $110.4m

○ $341.0m

---

44   Flavio Co, a European tyre manufacturer, is investigating the possible acquisition of a UK company. If this takes place, the acquisition will be complete within the next month.

As part of this investigation Flavio Co has obtained the following data:

Current spot rate: 1 GBP is currently worth 1.3501 EUR

Inflation forecast for the Eurozone: 0.75%

Inflation forecast for the UK: 1.25%

Using this data, which is the BEST estimate of the forecast value of a euro in one year, and the potential impact of this exchange rate movement on the outcome of this acquisition?

○   1.3568 unfavourable impact

○   0.7444 unfavourable impact

○   1.3568 favourable impact

○   0.7444 favourable impact

---

45   Crichton Co is preparing to acquire Slack Co in a share for share exchange.

Crichton Co currently has 100 million shares in issue, valued at $4 per share and Slack Co has 40 million shares in issue, valued at $2 per share.

Synergies totalling a present value of $24m post-tax are expected to be generated by the takeover.

The post-acquisition cost of capital is estimated to be 10%.

The corporate tax rate is 20%.

Crichton Co wants to generate an increase in its share price of at least 5% as a result of this acquisition.

What is the maximum share for share offer that is acceptable to Crichton?

O   1 Crichton Co share for 1.79 Slack Co shares

O   2 Crichton Co shares for 1 Slack Co share

O   1 Crichton Co share for 2 Slack Co shares

O   1 Crichton Co share for 2.12 Slack Co shares

---

46   Xyro Co intends to acquire Quantum Co via a 1 for 3 share for share exchange.

Xyro Co has 15m shares in issue with a total value (market capitalisation) of $120m, and generates annual earnings of $6m.

Quantum has 9m shares in issue with a total market capitalisation of $10.5m, and generates annual earnings of $1.5m.

An independent analyst has estimated that after the takeover Xyro's share price will rise by 10%, on the assumption that the P/E of the combined company is expected to be the same as Xyro's current P/E ratio.

The corporate tax rate is 20%.

What post-tax annual synergy is the analyst assuming in their calculations?

O $3.06m

O $0.42m

O $3.82m

O $0.53m

---

47   A large ungeared pharmaceutical company, Quark Co, is interested in acquiring a smaller research-based pharmaceutical company called Biotech. Biotech is forecast to make profits (before interest and tax) of $250,000 in the next financial year.

Information on potential ratios to use to value Biotech is given below:

•   Average earnings yield for listed companies = 8.3%

•   Average earnings yield for pharmaceutical companies = 12.5%

•   Average earnings yield for recently acquired research based pharmaceutical companies = 5%

The corporate tax rate is 20%.

Using the above information, what is the MOST appropriate value of Biotech?

O $2.4m

O $1.6m

O $5m

O $4m

---

48   Wagoo Co is interested in acquiring a smaller high-performing rival, Cramper Co which operates in a specific high-growth market niche. Wagoo Co hopes to sell the land and buildings worth $10m as a result of the acquisition and to increase its own earnings by 5% as a result of the acquisition.

Further information:

	Wagoo	Cramper
Earnings	$20m	$3m
P/E ratio	5	15

What is the maximum Wagoo Co should offer to Cramper's shareholders?

O $245.0m

O $160.0m

O $60.0m

O $115.0m

---

49   Smartbox Co and Deadeye Co are rival computer game developers, both companies are profitable.

Smartbox Co has a higher P/E of 20 compared to Deadeye Co's P/E of 10. However Deadeye Co's EPS is higher.

Smartbox and Deadeye have the same level of financial gearing (debt divided by equity based on market values).

Smartbox Co has made a takeover bid for Deadeye Co. The bid is a share-for-share offer of two Smartbox shares for three Deadeye Co shares. This has been calculated based on a P/E ratio of 15 for Deadeye Co.

Based on this information, which TWO of the following statements are MOST likely to be true?

☐   The share price of Smartbox will fall after the acquisition.

☐   Smartbox Co's gearing (calculated on market values of debt and equity) will be unaffected.

☐   The EPS will rise post-acquisition.

☐   Both sets of shareholders are likely to gain from the acquisition.

---

50   Pure Co is a large listed company which makes pharmaceutical products. Pure Co is planning to acquire Jurassic Co. Jurassic Co is a fast-growing unlisted drug discovery company which is managed by its current owners.

Which THREE of the following methods are MOST likely to reduce the risk of this acquisition to Pure Co?

☐   Involving banks in providing the main part of the finance for a cash bid, with the debt being secured on the assets of Jurassic Co

☐   Making the acquisition with a series of cash payments agreed in advance – with positive covenants attached

☐   A change of control clause on Jurassic Co' existing debt finance.

☐   Using convertible debt to make the purchase

☐   Using a mix of cash and paper to make the bid, instead of a cash bid

51   Blemish Co and Dry Co are both in the dry cleaning industry. Blemish Co has agreed to purchase Dry Co via a share for share exchange; the terms offered are two Dry Co shares for one Blemish Co share.

The expected synergies are likely to produce post-tax savings of $100,000 per year.

Blemish Co is assuming that the new entity will be valued on the same multiple of earnings that it currently has.

Blemish Co's latest EPS is $0.50 and its earnings yield is 4%. It has 2 million shares in issue.

Dry Co's latest EPS is $0.60 and its share price is $3.60. It has 1 million shares in issue.

The rate of corporate tax is 20%.

From the point of view of Dry Co's shareholders – how much is this offer worth?

○ $14.17

○ $7.08

○ $8.50

○ $17.0

---

52   Smorgasbord Co (S Co) is a multinational drinks business. S Co has decided to dispose of its wine division by selling it via a Management Buyout (MBO).

The management team of the wine division believe that it has good prospects, and despite being loss making at present could be turned around and listed on the local stock market in approximately five years.

S Co have valued the division at $37 million, consisting of $10 million of tangible assets and $27 million of estimated intangible asset value. The division would be sold free of any debt. Gearing levels in the wine industry are normally very low (often zero) because of the volatility of the cash flows in this industry.

The management of the wine division can raise $5 million from their own resources.

The managers of the wine division have approached a venture capitalist to provide the rest of the finance via a mix of types of finance.

What is the MOST likely finance structure that would be acceptable to the venture capitalist and the management team?

○ $5.0m of equity/$10m debt/$10m of convertible non-cumulative preference shares

○ $10.0m of equity/$10m debt/$12m of convertible non-cumulative preference shares

○ $5.0m of equity/$10m debt/$17m of convertible non-cumulative preference shares

○ $10.0m of equity/$2m debt/$20m of convertible non-cumulative preference shares

---

53   Company A is in the process of making an offer to acquire Company B. The proposed offer is for one new share in Company A for every two shares held in Company B.

Company A has 200 million shares currently trading at $4 each; Company B has 100 million shares trading at $1.50 each.

Company A has estimated that the present value of the synergies arising on a successful acquisition will be $40 million.

Assume that the shares prices given have not yet moved to anticipate the takeover.

What is the BEST estimate of the expected value of a share in the combined company post-acquisition?

- ○ $3.80
- ○ $3.30
- ○ $3.96
- ○ $2.48

---

54   Asparagus Co is a wholesale company supplying fresh fruit and vegetables to supermarkets in Country Z. Following a recent review of Asparagus Co's capital structure, the directors are planning to introduce more debt into the capital structure in order to take further advantage of the tax savings on debt finance.

Asparagus Co currently has 40m shares in issue valued at $2.50/share and a 5% undated bond with a market value of $50m.

A new 4% bond will be issued and the proceeds will be used to repurchase 25% of Asparagus Co's shares at their current market value.

The corporate tax rate is 20%.

What will be the share price of Asparagus Co after the bond issue and share repurchase?

$ [   ]   to two decimal places.

---

55   A venture capitalist has just received a request from a team of managers who are attempting to finance a management buy out (MBO).

In assessing this request which of the following is likely to be the LEAST important in influencing the decision of the venture capitalist in whether to participate in the MBO:

- ○   Information on the MBO's management team – their experience, achievements and qualifications.
- ○   Management accounts from the current owners showing the profits of the entity being bought for the past two years.
- ○   Cash flow forecasts for the MBO for the next five years.
- ○   Information on the growth potential of the industry that the MBO operates in.

---

56 **What £/$ exchange rate would be predicted for a year in the future using interest rate parity?**

The current spot rate is £1 = $1.5000.

Annual interest rates are currently 2.0% in the UK and 4% in the USA.

£1 = $

to four decimal places.

---

57 **Which of the following statements about interest rate risk is true?**

O   An interest rate floor can be used to hedge an expected increase in interest rates.

O   The cost of an interest rate floor is higher than the cost of an interest rate collar.

O   The premium on an interest rate option is payable when it is exercised.

O   The standardised nature of interest rate futures means that over- and under-hedging can be avoided.

---

58 A company that has a $10m loan with a variable rate of interest, has entered into a forward rate agreement (FRA) with a financial institution that offered a 3–6, 3.2%–2.7% spread.

What would be the payment made to the financial institution under the terms of the FRA if the actual rate of interest was 3%?

$ | | to the nearest dollar.

---

59 Company Z's domestic currency is the dollar. It has recently begun exporting to a European country and expects to receive €500,000 in six months' time. The company plans to take action to hedge the exchange rate risk arising from its European exports.

Company Z could put cash on deposit in the European country at an annual interest rate of 3% per year, and borrow at 5% per year. The company could put cash on deposit in its home country at an annual interest rate of 4% per year, and borrow at 6% per year.

The following exchange rates are currently available to Company Z:

Current spot exchange rate   2.000 euro per $
Six-month forward exchange rate   1.990 euro per $

Company Z wants to hedge its future euro receipt.

What is the dollar value of a money market hedge in six months' time?

$ | | to the nearest whole dollar.

---

60 The forward rate is 0.8500–0.8650 euros to the $.

What will a €2,000 receipt be converted to at the forward rate?

O $1,730

O $2,312

O $2,353

O $1,700

BPP
LEARNING
MEDIA

Practice mock answers

Answers

1   The correct answer is: **20.9%.**

The question does not tell us what the share price has been over the period, but it does provide the price/earnings (P/E) ratio. We can derive the share price as follows:

	Previous year	*Current year*
Share price	17 × 5,100/9,000 = 9.63	18 × 5,700/9,000 = 11.40
Dividend yield		(2,200/9,000)/9.63 = 2.5%

Total shareholder return (TSR) = 0.025 + (11.40 − 9.63)/9.63 = 0.209 or 20.9%

Note that the share price at the end of the previous year is the share price at the start of the current year, and it is this figure that is used in the TSR calculation.

If you calculated the answer to be 17.7% then you used the end of year share price.

If you calculated the answer to be 18.2% then you only considered the capital gain.

2   The correct answer is: **Exchange rate: A\$/B\$ 2.41, sales objective met.**

Forecast spot rate = 2.5 × (1.02/1.06) = 2.41

Income from country B = B\$25 million/2.41 = A\$ 10,373,444, therefore meeting their objective of generating A\$10 million in revenue from sales to Country B in one year's time.

If you calculated an exchange rate of 2.60, you incorrectly applied IRP as 2.5 × (1.06/1.02) = 2.60.

3   The correct answer is: **Gearing is 92.6% and the thin capitalisation rules are breached.**

Book value of debt	=	\$200m
Book value of equity	=	\$216m (W)
Therefore gearing	=	\$200m/\$216m = 92.6% which exceeds the limit of 85% and therefore the covenant is breached.

Working

Share capital	=	\$100m
Retained earnings	=	\$116m
Retained earnings b/f =		\$100m

Retained earnings in 20X2:

Operating profit	60
Interest @ 10% (\$200m @ 10%)	(20)
PBT	40
Tax @ 20%	(8)
PFY	32
Retained @ 50%	16

Therefore retained earnings at 20X2	=	\$100m + \$16m	=	\$116m
Total equity	=	\$100m + \$116m	=	\$216m

If you calculated gearing as 68.75% this is incorrectly based on market values:

Equity	=	\$200m/\$100	=	2m × \$110m	=	\$220m
Gearing	=	100 million shares × SP \$3.20	=	\$320m		
Gearing	=	220/320	=	68.75%		
SP	=	10 × \$0.32	=	\$3.20		

4   The correct answer is: **Minimising the cost per sq metre of property rental costs.**

Property rental costs are a key input to a business of any type, economy is concerned with minimising the cost of inputs and therefore this is an economy measure.

Keeping spending within budget relates inputs to outputs and this is a characteristic of efficiency targets.

Minimising the percent of spending on admin costs an example of efficiency targets because it relates to the use of 'inputs'.

The cost of dealing with a customer complaint is another efficiency measure because it relates cost to the resolution of a complaint (ie it is another input–output measure).

- • The financial gearing of a company
    - – This can be measured by a ratio that compares net debt to equity, not EBITDA
- • How many times the earnings could pay the interest
    - – This is similar to interest cover (but this compares interest to PBIT, not earnings)

5   The correct answer is: **24%**

	Current	Forecast	Change
Sales	$5.5m	5.225 (5.5 × 0.95)	
Op profit	$0.825 (5.5 × 0.15)	0.627 (5.225 × 0.12)	0.198 being 24% (0.198/0.25)

3% is simply the fall in operating margin

20% is the percentage decrease in operating margin (3%/15%)

5% is the percentage decrease in sales

6   The correct answer is: **28%**

($0.50 + $0.20)/$2.50 = 28%

$0.50 is the capital gain on the share ($3–$2.50)

7   The correct answer is: **Interest cover covenant not breached, debt/(cash flow from operations) covenant not breached.**

Interest cover:

Operating profit	= $4m × 1.2	= $4.8m
Interest	= ($10m × 10%) + ($5m × 12%)	= $1.6m
Interest cover	= $4.8m/$1.6m	= 3

Covenant is an interest cover limit of 2.5, therefore the interest cover needs to exceed 2.5 which it does.

Covenant not breached.

Debt/(cash flow from operations):

Debt	= $10m + $5m	= $15m
Cash flow from operations	= $5m × 1.15	= $5.75m
Debt/(cash flow from operations)	= $15m/$5.75m	= 2.6

Covenant is a limit of 3 therefore Debt/(Cash flow from operations) needs to be **below** 3 which it is.

Covenant not breached.

8   The correct answers are:

Financial capital relates to the pool of funds that is available to an organisation for use in the production of goods or services, **eg cash in bank.**

Manufactured capital relates to the manufactured physical objects available for use in the production of goods or the provision of services. **None of the items here relate to this type of capital.**

Intellectual capital relates to organisational knowledge-based intangibles. **None of the items here relate to this type of capital.**

Human capital relates to people's competencies, capabilities and experience, and their motivations to innovate – **the staff engagement survey relates to this.**

Social and relationship capital relates to the institutions and the relationships within and between communities, groups of stakeholders and other networks, and the ability to share information to enhance individual and collective well-being **including the brand and reputation that an organisation has developed.**

Natural capital relates to renewable and non-renewable environmental resources and processes, **eg improvements in CO_2 emissions.**

9   The correct answer is: **Share price $57.143 after buyback.**

Buyback analysis:

Franco Co is currently worth 400,000 (shares) × $50 (share price) = **$20m.**

After the buyback the company is worth $20m – $2.5m = $17.5m.

The number of shares bought back is 50,000 ($2.5m / $50), so 350,000 shares remain.

The share price becomes $17.5m / 350,000 = $50.

Wealth after share buyback =

(875 shares × $50 share price) + (125 shares sold × $50 received per share) = $50,000

10   The correct answers are:

- **Lower EPS.**
- **Higher market capitalisation.**

More shares in issue will dilute EPS.

Although shareholder wealth will not be affected, the decision to retain cash within the company by using a scrip dividend should mean that the overall value of the company's shares are higher.

Notes on incorrect answers:

- A higher P/E ratio
    - More shares in issue will dilute the share price and the EPS by the same amount (eg double the amount of shares in issue leads to a halving of Price and EPS) so there is no impact on the P/E ratio, in theory of a scrip issue.
- Higher gearing (calculated using book values)
    - A scrip dividend has no impact on the book value of equity or debt. A cash dividend will reduce retained earnings (part of the book value of equity) and therefore increases gearing compared to a scrip issue.

11   The correct answer is: **10.0**

Dividends and earnings are growing by 9.5% per year.

Dividends are consistently 5% of earnings so 95% of earnings are being re-invested.

If g = r × b then 0.095 = r × 0.95

So r = 0.095 / 0.95 = 0.1 or **10.0%.**

BPP
LEARNING
MEDIA

12   The correct answers are:

- **Leaving the dividend unchanged.**
- **Issuing a bond to raise the required finance.**

Leaving the dividend unchanged may be appropriate if combined with issuing a bond. This would allow Francis Co to raise the finance required without employing equity finance.

Abandoning the expansion plan may put the Francis Co's strategy at risk – the plan is predicted to give a return well above the company's WACC and should therefore create wealth for shareholders as long as it is not equity financed (the IRR is below the cost of equity). For this reason a rights issue is not appropriate. Cutting the dividend is not advisable as dividend payments have just recently commenced and may be expected by investors.

13   The correct answer is: **Wizz Co's share price will be diluted as a result of the proposed stock split.**

A 1 for 1 stock split involves reducing the par value of a Wizz Co share by half and thereby doubling the number of shares in issue. There will be no change to the total amount of equity (so no impact on gearing). However, doubling the number of shares is likely to reduce the share price (despite the attractive returns from the projects) – although this is not the same thing as reducing shareholder wealth.

The proposed policies are consistent with the objective of shareholder wealth maximisation because the expected project return of 20% is above the required shareholder return of 14.8% (calculated as $4 + (10 - 4) \times 1.8$).

14   The correct answer is: **25%**

Earnings yield = EPS / share price

So earnings yield × share price = earnings per share

Dividend cover = earnings / dividends

So earnings per share / dividend cover = dividend per share

	20X7	20X5
Earnings yield (EY)	5.0%	10.0%
Share price (SP)	6.00	2.00
EY × SP = EPS	0.30	0.20
Dividend cover (DC)	3.0	2.5
EPS / DC = dividend per share	0.10	0.08

Growth = (0.1 – 0.8) / 0.8 × 100 = 25%

15   The correct answers are:

- **The scrip dividend will create pressure on dividends per share in the future.**
- **The clientèle effect suggests the private equity company will be dissatisfied.**

The scrip dividend puts more shares in issue, so if dividend per share is to grow then more dividends in $ millions will have to be paid. The private equity firm is presumably happy with the dividend policy of VJ and changing this may cause problems – this is consistent with the idea of the clientele effect.

Notes on incorrect answers:

- Pecking-order theory suggest that the founding family will continue to want cash dividends.

  – The family may prefer to have cash dividends but this is not linked to pecking order theory. Pecking-order theory suggests that the first capital to use is cash in hand, so this would be consistent with the idea of **scrapping** the cash dividend.

- Abandoning a cash dividend will send a negative signal affecting VJ's share price.
    - VJ is not a listed company and therefore does not have a share price.

16   The correct answer is: **Increasing the gearing ratio will decrease the WACC and increase the value of the entity.**

An increase in gearing will reduce the WACC as debt is a cheaper source of finance and brings additional tax relief to the company. A company's value is a reflection of the future present value of its cash flows. So the lower the WACC then the higher the value of the total capital of the entity (debt + equity).

17   The correct answer is: **16.2%**

$K_{eg} = 12 + (12 - 6) \times 1 \times (0.7) = 12 + 4.2 = 16.2\%$

18   The correct answer is: **Financial statements of Drilbit Co for the last three years.**

Future performance will be critical to bank's analysis. The environmental impact of a new oil field can give rise to huge financial liabilities as BP's experience has shown.

19   The correct answer is: **Eurobonds can be issued without granting security.**

This is a powerful general advantage of Eurobonds over other forms of debt finance.

Notes on incorrect answers:

- Lower interest rates in the USA.
    - This is a possible advantage, but over the long-term this is likely to be associated with low inflation in the USA and therefore a stronger $. This will make the Eurobonds more expensive to service.
- To reduce its cost of capital.
    - This is a motive for issuing any form of debt, but not specifically Eurobonds.
- Eurobonds are often less expensive because they can only be issued by companies with a high credit rating.
    - This is true for any form of debt issue, an excellent credit rating always helps: it is the lack of regulation of the Eurobond market that may make it cheaper than a domestic bond issue.

20   The correct answer is: **5.15%.**

Unless otherwise stated the variable leg of an interest rate swap takes place at LIBOR. Here the swap involves Lenny Co paying interest at a fixed rate and receiving at a variable rate (ie LIBOR).

The bank makes its profit from the swap from the difference between the bid and the offer rate – it receives the higher rate (here 4.15%).

So Lenny Co pays interest at 4.15% (the swap), pays interest LIBOR + 1% (on its loan) and receives the variable swap rate at LIBOR. Its net cost is therefore 5.15%.

21   The correct answers are:

- **The cost of capital.**
- **The tax calculation of 152,000.**

The cost of capital should be the **post-tax cost of the loan**, ie 8% × (1 – t) = 6%.

The tax calculation ignores the tax relief on the lease payment which is claimed in time 1 and received in time 2 (through to time 6).

The outlay represents the present value of the loan – and this is saved if the lease is taken out.

BPP
LEARNING
MEDIA

22   The correct answer is: **1 for 4 at an issue price of $4.**

The issue price will be $5 × 0.8 = $4.

The amount raised will be $4.5m / 0.9 = $5m.

To raise $5m at $4/share requires 5m/4 = 1.25m new shares.

There are 5m shares in issue so the required rights issue is 1.25m for 5m, ie 1 for 4.

Notes on the incorrect answers:

$ 4.80 is the TERP.

A 1 for 5 issue results from incorrectly deducting the issue costs from the amounts raised.

23   The correct answer is: **Interest would be 0.5% lower.**

Floating rate finance plus the swap would give an outcome of:

Pay floating rate on finance = L + 1%

Pay fixed on swap = 4.5% (being the higher of the two rates quoted)

Receive LIBOR on swap.

Therefore net impact is L + 1% + 4.5% – L = 5.5%.

Compared to 6% on fixed-rate finance this gives a saving of 0.5%.

24   The correct answer is: **1.60.**

Shareholders who apply to buy shares at a higher price will also be able to buy shares at a lower price, if a lower price is chosen. So the results of the tender prices are as follows:

Tender price	Shares requested (at this price)	Total new shares	Total finance
$1.40	100 million	200m	$280m (20 + 30 + 50 + 100)
$1.60	50 million	100m	$160m (20 + 30 + 50)
$1.80	30 million	50m	$90m (20 + 30)
$2.00	20 million	20m	$40m

Mr Croft currently owns 0.75 × 200 = 150m shares. So the maximum number of shares in issue after the tender offer will need to be 300m for Mr Croft's minimum ownership criteria to be met. This means that a maximum of 100m new shares can be issued (because there are 200m before the tender offer). The highest amount of cash raised without breaching this limit is achieved at $1.60.

25   The correct answer is: **$5.3**

The issue price of the new shares will be $5 × (1 − 0.36) = $3.20.

So the number of shares that Osgood will need to issue to finance this venture is $8m / 3.2 = 2.5 million.

Given that there are 8 million shares in issue this is a 2.5 : 8 or 1: 3.2 rights issue, we can now use the formula for the yield-adjusted ex rights price, where:

N	= 3.2
Cum rights price	= $5
Issue price	= $3.20
Ynew	= 0.30
Yold	= 0.15

Yield-adjusted TERP = [1/4.2] [(3.2 × 5) + 3.2 × 0.3 / 0.15]

$\qquad\qquad\qquad\quad$ = 0.238 × [16 + 6.4]

$\qquad\qquad\qquad\quad$ = **5.3 (to one decimal place)**

An alternative approach is as follows:

Before share issue	8m shares	8m × $5	= Value $40m
Share issue	2.5m shares	2.5m × $3.2 × 30/15	= Value $16m
Total	10.5m shares		Value $56m

Yield-adjusted TERP = $56m / 10.5m = $5.3 (to one decimal place).

26   The correct answers are:

- **If the investment is regarded as low risk and is expected to create reliable cash inflows.**
- **If interest cover at Fenchurch Co is already well above the industry norm.**

If the investment creates reliable cash inflows as seems likely here then the investment is more suitable for debt finance because the cash flows from the investment are stable and are highly likely to more than cover the costs of the debt repayments.

If interest cover is high then the existing debt that Fenchurch has is affordable and Fenchurch therefore is likely to have the capacity to take on more debt finance.

Notes on incorrect answers:

- If Fenchurch is a listed company then raising any finance, whether debt or equity, should be more feasible.
- Companies sometimes use debt finance to minimise the number of shares in issue, and this could be a reason for the high EPS. If this was the case then further issues of debt may not be welcomed by shareholders or by other stakeholders.

BPP
LEARNING
MEDIA

27   The correct answer is: **If taxes are zero then the value an entity will be the same at any level of gearing.**

M&M theory suggests that the WACC will fall (and so the value of an entity will rise) due to tax savings. Without tax savings the WACC and corporate value are unaffected by changes in gearing.

Notes on incorrect answers:

- The value of a corporate entity will rise as gearing rises but only up to the optimal level of gearing – if taxes are zero corporate value (debt + equity) is unaffected by changes in gearing.

- The cost of equity increases as gearing increases up to a certain level of gearing and then falls.

  - By any theory this is not true, the cost of equity will ALWAYS rise as gearing rises because higher debt levels increase financial risk.

- There is potentially more than one optimal level of gearing - with M&M theory if taxes are zero then there is no such thing as optimal gearing.

28   The correct answer is: **$52,800**

Time	CF $'000	DF @ 4% (5% × (1 − 0.2))	PV $'000
0–5	(12,000)	5.452 (w1)	(65,424)
1–6	2,400	5.242	12,581
			52,843

W1

DF1–5 = 4.452

DF0 = 1

Therefore DF0–5 = 5.452.

29   The correct answer is: **The gearing used is incorrect.**

The correct formula has been used.

The error is that if the gearing ratio is defined as debt / equity then 20% gearing means 20 of gearing for every 100 of equity. So the error is that the figure of 80 for V_e should be 100.

30   The correct answer is: **10.75%.**

The adjusted cost of equity can be calculated using M&M's formula for the cost of equity, where:

$$K_{eg} = K_{eu} = (K_{eu} - K_d)\ \frac{V_d(1 - t)}{V_e}$$

K_{eu} = 0.1

K_d = 0.05

t = 0.25

V_d = 0.2 (representing 20% gearing)

V_e = 1.00 (the debt to equity ratio is 20% so there is 20 of debt to 100 of equity)

K_{eg} = 0.1 + (0.1 − 0.05) 0.2 (1 − 0.25) / 1.00 = 0.1075 or **10.75%**

Notes on incorrect answers:

If you calculated the answer to be 10.94% then you have calculated V_d as 0.2 and V_e as 0.8. This would be correct if the gearing of 20% in the question had been defined as debt / (debt + equity).

If you calculated the answer to be 9.58% or 9.50% then you have attempted to use the M&M formula for the WACC – but this is not asked for here.

31   The correct answers are:

- **Smart Co's beta is likely to rise.**
- **Synergies are likely.**
- **Smart's EPS will rise post-acquisition.**

The use of debt finance will mean that gearing will rise post-acquisition, so Smart's beta will rise. EPS will rise because Sunshine is profitable and no more shares are being issued. Synergies are likely because both companies are in similar sectors, so for example they will have higher buying power over their suppliers.

Notes on incorrect answers:

- Smart's WACC is likely to rise.

  - This may happen but depends on Smart Co's current gearing. M&M with tax suggests that the WACC should fall if more debt finance is taken on. and the impact of further.

- Smart Co's cost of equity is likely to fall due to the reduced competition and therefore less risk in this sector.

  - The cost of equity will rise due to the increase in gearing. The reduction in competition will be minimal because the two businesses operate in different sectors of the market anyway.

32   The correct answers are:

- **Venture capitalists would expect a set on the board and to be involved in key decisions.**

- **Venture capitalists would normally expect an exit route within a period of less than 10 years.**

- **Venture capital finance is expensive and may prove too expensive for Company A to finance.**

Incorrect answers:

- Venture capitalists will require an equity stake of at least 50% to ensure they have control of the company.

- Venture capitalists provide only equity finance and would not provide a mix of debt and equity.

33   The correct answer is: **$2.66m.**

A P/E ratio of 15 means that Echo's earnings must be the share price divided by 15, ie $3 / 15 = $0.2 per share. Total earnings are therefore $0.2 × 8m = $1.6m.

Preference share dividends are 0.04 × $1 × 10m = $0.4m.

Remember that there is no tax relief on preference dividends, ie they are paid out of post-tax profits.

So profits after tax are $1.6m + $0.4m = $2m.

Pre-tax this is $2m / 0.8 = $2.5m.

Echo's interest payments are $0.4m. This can be calculated in one of two ways:

1   Coupon rate × book value: 0.04 × $4m = $0.16m
2   Expected return × market value: 0.037 × $4.32m = $0.16m

So profits **before interest** and tax = $2.5 + $0.16m = **$2.66m**.

34   The correct answer is: **$219m**

The minimum value of a listed company will be the current value of its shares (its market capitalisation). This is what the shares can be sold for on the open market.

If the stock market is efficient then this reinforces the meaning of this value.

The realisable value of the assets is a minimum value for an UNLISTED company.

35   The correct answer is: **$300m**

The dividend valuation model can be applied here.

Growth can be estimated using r × b.

Dividend payout = 12/20 = 0.6 so b = 1 − 0.6 = 0.4

r = 0.15

So g = 0.15 × 0.4 = 0.06

Using the dividend valuation model $P_0 = d_1 \times (1 / (K_e - g))$

$P_0 = 12 \times (1 / (0.10 - 0.06)) = $300m$

Note that the next dividend of $12m is given and so you do not have to apply the growth rate to calculate d_1 in this case.

36   The correct answers are:

- **Use of a free cash flow to equity approach based on a cost of equity that is higher than 10% to reflect the need to compensate shareholders for Denhelm's higher than average risk.**

- **Use of the P/E ratio of 14.**

- **Use of the P/E ratio of less than 14 to reflect the impact of Denhelm's structure.**

Denhelms' higher financial risk would argue for the use of a **lower** P/E ratio or a **higher** cost of equity. Both of these reduce Denhelm's value to reflect its high risk (due to its size and gearing).

Use of the industry average P/E of 14 may be justified due to the listing **changing** the gearing and size of Denhelm Co.

The other approaches will not work here:

- Use of the dividend valuation model – this won't work because the growth rate is above the K_e so this will produce a negative number.

- Use of the P/E ratio of 15 – this is the stock market average and is not directly relevant to Denhelm Co's growth prospects or risk.

- Use of a higher P/E than 14 to reflect the need to compensate shareholders for Denhelm's higher than average risk – this would have the effect of increasing the value of Denhelm to reflect higher risk. This is not correct as discussed above.

37 The correct answer is: **Valuing the tangible assets (using realisable values) and intangible assets (using CIV) of Byfly.**

ByFly has a sufficient track record to be able to estimate the value of its intangibles using CIV and also has valuable tangible assets.

The other methods will be more difficult to apply here:

- The P/E method will only be possible if ByFly Co is making profits after interest and tax. Currently it is loss making.

- Dividends are irregular and unpredictable – so the dividend valuation model is unlikely to be useful.

- The earnings yield method again will only be possible if ByFly Co is making profits after interest and tax. Currently it is loss making.

38 The correct answers are:

- **The 6% average dividend growth rate is unlikely to be reflective of future dividend growth.** This is true given that the investment is in a project with very high growth potential.

- **Using the industry average asset beta in CAPM is incorrect.** This is true, given that the company is geared, the equity beta should be used in CAPM.

- **It is inaccurate to assume that the dividend growth rate will be constant.** This is true due to the new high-growth project and investment from the VC.

The incorrect answers are:

- The dividend valuation model should only be used to value a controlling interest. This is not true, the model should be used only to value a minority interest

- CAPM cannot be used to estimate the cost of equity of an unlisted company. This is not true, CAPM can be used with an appropriate beta factor that reflects risk of the unlisted company.

39 The correct answer is: **1123.60.**

Historic growth can be estimated by comparing the latest dividend of 53 cents to the dividend three years ago of 44.50 cents.

$$g = \sqrt[3]{\frac{53}{44.5}} - 1 = 0.06$$

So the price of a share can be estimated using the dividend valuation model.

$$P_0 = \frac{d_1}{K_e - g}$$

d_1 = next dividend = $53 \times 1.06 = 56.18$.

So $P_0 = \dfrac{56.18}{0.11 - 0.06} = 1123.60$ cents.

Note on incorrect answers:

If you calculate the average growth rate over four years (an easy mistake because there are headings for four years) then you will have calculated the answer to be approximately 847.92. This is incorrect because there are three years of growth **between** 20X4 and 20X7.

The other answers can be obtained if you mistakenly use the current dividend (d_0) instead of the forecast dividend (d_1) in the dividend valuation formula.

BPP
LEARNING
MEDIA

Answers **161**

40   The correct answers are:

- **The valuation is likely to be understated as forecast future growth has been ignored beyond Year 3.** Correct – expected future growth beyond Year 3 should be built into the calculations and will increase the valuation of Company B.

- **The valuation is understated as the directors have failed to include a perpetuity factor in the calculations.** Correct – Company B wold be expected to continue to operate into the foreseeable future and therefore a perpetuity factor should be built into the calculations.

- **The approach used calculates the value of the total entity not the value of equity.** Correct – the value of debt would need to be deducted to calculate the value of equity.

Incorrect answers:

- The valuation is overstated as the directors have failed to deduct tax from the free cash flows. Incorrect – free cash flow to all investors is already net of tax.

- Free cash flows to all investors should be discounted at 10% being the cost of equity and not 8% being WACC.

- Incorrect – FCF to all investors included both cash flows available to equity and debt investors and therefore should be discounted at WACC, not cost of equity.

41   The correct answer is: **$2.43.**

T_1 = 250,000 × 0.926 = $231,500

T_2 = 250,000 × 0.857 = $214,250

T_3 onwards:

250,000 × 1.03/(0.08-0.03) = $5,150,000 × 0.857 ($T_2$ DF) = 4,413,550

Total value = 231,500 + 214,250 + 4,413,550 = 4,859,300/2,000,000 shares = $2.43

Distractors:

$2.27 – incorrectly uses the T_3 discount factor for the period of constant growth:

250,000 × 1.03/(0.08-0.03) = $5,150,000 × 0.794(T3 DF) = 4,089,100 + 214,250 + 231,500 = 4,534,850/2,000,000 = $2.27

$2.21 – this ignores the first two years where there is no growth: 4,413,500/2,000,000 = $2.21.

$2.58 – this uses the 3% growth from T_1.

250,000 × 1.03/(0.08-0.03) = $5,150,000/2,000,000 = $2.58

42   The correct answer is: **$100,000.**

Net assets = $600,000 (1,750,000 – 1,150,000)

Less write down of NCA $400,000 (650,000 – 250,000)

Less write down of inventory $100,000

Incorrect answers:

$1,250,000 – incorrectly using net assets of $1,750,000 (which is total assets) less write-down for NCA and inventory ($500,000).

$600,000 – this is net assets with no adjustments (therefore the book value asset valuation).

$250,000 – this uses net assets of $600,000 and incorrectly adjusts for the NCA write down of $250,000 (being NRV instead of the difference between NRV and NBV) and inventory of $100,000.

43 The correct answer is: **$210.4m.**

We assume that the cash flows are after interest (because they are post tax) the cost of debt is already taken into account so the cost of equity needs to be used as the discount factor.

Time	1	2	
$m	15.0	17.5	
df 11%	0.901	0.812	
PV	13.5	14.2	Total = $27.7m

The cash flows **after time 2** need to be discounted in two stages.

Step 1 : from the perspective of **time 2** – as a growing annuity discounted at $(1 / (K_e - g))$ ie $(1 / (0.11 - 0.03) = 12.5$

After time 2

18.0   (calculated as 17.5×1.03)

df	12.5
PV at time 2	225.0

Step 2: discounted this back to a time 0 value, using a time 2 discount factor at 11% (Ke)

Time 2

225.0

df	0.812
PV at time 0	182.7

Finally the total PV of Spearman Co's cash flows can be calculated:

PV of cash flows from time 1–2	=	$27.7m
PV of cash flows after time 2	=	$182.7m
Total	=	$210.4m

This is the total PV of the entity's cash flows after financing costs.

Notes on incorrect answers:

If you calculated the answer to be $252.7m then you have forgotten to discount the post time 2 cash flows back to a present value.

If your answer was $110.4m you have incorrectly deducted the market value of debt (which would be the correct approach IF the cash flows had been given BEFORE interest).

If you calculated $341m you have discounted the cash flows at the WACC (which would be the correct approach IF the cash flows had been given BEFORE interest).

44 The correct answer is: **0.7444 unfavourable impact.**

Using the purchasing power parity theory formula:

$$S_1 = S_0 \times \frac{1 + r_{var}}{1 + r_{base}}$$

S_0 = value of a euro today = $1 / 1.3501 = 0.7407$

R_{var} = inflation in UK = 0.0125

R_{base} = inflation in Eurozone = 0.0075

$S_1 = 0.7407 \times 1.0125 / 1.0075 = 0.7444$

A stronger euro means a weaker £ (GBP) and this is likely to be unfavourable because the assets and profits of the UK company will be worth less in euros.

45   The correct answer is: **1 Crichton Co share for 2 Slack Co shares.**

Post-acquisition value = Value of Crichton + Value of Slack + Value of synergies

Value of Crichton = 100m shares × $4 = $400m

Value of Slack = 40m shares × $2 = $80m

Value of synergies = $24m (given)

So post-acquisition value = $400m + $80m + $24m = **$504m**

Required post-acquisition share price = $4 × 1.05 = **$4.20**

So required number of shares post-acquisition = $504m / $4.20 = 120m

So max number of new shares = 120m – 100m existing shares = 20m

20m Crichton shares for 40m Slack shares = 1 for 2.

Note. The answer of 1 for 1.79 is obtained if the cost of capital is applied to calculate the present value of synergies, ie 24 × 1/0.1 = $240m. This type of analysis is only needed if the synergies are given per annum, here the present value of the synergies is provided directly in the question.

The answer of 1 for 2.12 is obtained if the present value of the synergies are adjusted by multiplying by (1 – t). This type of analysis is only needed if the synergies are given pre-tax, here the present value of the synergies post-tax is provided directly in the question.

46   The correct answer is: **$0.42m.**

Pre-acquisition share price is $120m / 15m = **$8**

Post-acquisition share price = $8 × 1.1 = **$8.8**

New shares issued = 9m divided by 3 (1 for 3 offer) = 3m

So post-acquisition no. of shares = 15m + 3m = **18m**

Total post-acquisition value = 18m × $8.8 = $158.4m

Earnings post-acquisition = Post-acquisition value of $158.4m divided by P/E of 20 (calculated as $120m / $6m) = $7.92m

Earnings pre-acquisition of Xyro + Quantum = $6m + $1.5m = $7.5m

Assumed synergy = $7.92m – $7.5m = $0.42m post-tax

Note. Pre-tax synergy = $0.42 / (1-t) = $0.75m / 0.8 = $0.53m

Note concerning the other incorrect answers:

The other incorrect answers result from a failure to adjust the no. of shares for the impact of the share for share offer, ie total no. of shares post acquisition is incorrectly calculated as 15m + 9m = 24m.

47   The correct answer is: **$4m.**

Earnings yield is earnings / price, ie the inverse of the P/E ratio.

The latest earnings yield for acquired research companies is low (this is like a P/E ratio being high and indicates high growth expectations; this the most suitable basis for valuing Biotech.

Biotech's post tax earnings are $250,000 × (1 – t) = $0.25m × 0.8 = $0.2m

Earnings × P/E = $0.2m × 1 / 0.05 = **$4m**

Notes on incorrect answers:

$5m is obtained if the pre-tax profit figure is used – remember earnings are **post-tax!**

The other answers are calculated using the incorrect earnings yield figures.

48   The correct answer is: **$60.0m.**

Post-acquisition value = post-acquisition value of Wagoo + post-acquisition of Cramper + synergy.

Separate P/E ratios will need to be used for each because they operate in slightly different markets.

Post-acquisition earnings of Wagoo = ($20m × 1.05) = $21m

P/E valuation of Wagoo post-acquisition = $21m × 5 = $105m

P/E valuation of Cramper = $3m × 15 = $45m

Synergy = $10m one-off asset sales

Total value = $105m + $45m + $10m = **$160m**

Wagoo's current value = $20m × 5 = $100m

Increase in value = $160m - $100m = **$60m**

This is the maximum Wagoo Co should offer to Cramper.

Notes on incorrect answers:

$245.0m is obtained if the whole of post-acquisition earnings are valued at a P/E of 15.

$160.0m is the post-acquisition value of the whole group.

$115.0m is calculated using the P/E ratio of the bidding company (P/E of 5) – this is not appropriate where the P/E of the bidder is **lower** than that of the company being acquired. Using a lower P/E ratio for the whole group would imply the acquisition lowers the growth prospects of the company being acquired, this is not logical.

49   The correct answers are:

- **The EPS will rise post-acquisition.**
- **Both sets of shareholders are likely to gain from the acquisition.**

This is an example of bootstrapping – where a company with a high P/E ratio buys a company in the same sector with a lower P/E ratio and turns it around. Here a company with a high EPS will be turned around so that it has the P/E of the bidder, ie approximately 20. If this company is bought on a P/E ratio of 15 this will boost the wealth of Smartbox (because after the takeover it will command a P/E of 20) and also of Deadeye (because before the takeover the company had a P/E of 10).

EPS will rise because Deadeye has a high EPS and has been acquired at a relatively low price.

Notes on incorrect answers:

- The share price of Smartbox will fall after the acquisition – this is unlikely as discussed above.

- Smartbox Co's gearing (calculated on market values of debt and equity) will be unaffected – because the market value of equity will rise (see above) the post-acquisition gearing of the company (using market values) should fall.

50   The correct answers are:

- **Involving banks in providing the main part of the finance for a cash bid, with the debt being secured on the assets of Jurassic Co.**

- **Making the acquisition with a series of cash payments agreed in advance – with positive covenants attached.**

- **Using a mix of cash and paper to make the bid, instead of a cash bid.**

BPP
LEARNING
MEDIA

Making the acquisition with a series of cash payments agreed in advance, with positive covenants attached, is called an earn-out agreement and reduces risk by retaining and incentivising the existing management team.

Using a mix of cash and paper to make the bid, instead of a cash bid – this again gives an incentive to the owner managers of Jurassic Co to make a success of the acquisition to increase the value of the Pure Co shares that they now own.

Involving banks in providing the main part of the finance for a cash bid, with the debt being secured on the assets of Jurassic Co – this is a leverage buy-out. The primary purpose of a leveraged buyout is to maximise the returns made by Pure Co on the equity that they are investing. However, it also has the effect of reducing the financial commitment being made by Pure Co and so could be argued to have a risk-reducing element (even though it increases the financial risk of Jurassic Co by increasing its gearing).

Notes on incorrect answers:

- A change of control clause on Jurassic Co' existing debt finance.

    - This will require Jurassic Co's debt to be repaid in full and will therefore increase the financial commitment being taken on by Pure Co.

- Using convertible debt to make the purchase.

    - This will reduce the risk to Jurassic's shareholders because they can convert the debt into shares if the acquisition is a success. However this is not a benefit to Pure Co.

51   The correct answer is: **$8.50.**

Blemish Co's P/E ratio indicates its growth prospects. Earnings yield = EPS / Price so the P/E ratio is 1/ earnings yield = 1 / 0.04 = 25.

The combined earnings of the company post-acquisition will be $1m for Blemish Co ($0.5 × 2m) plus $0.6m for Dry Co ($0.6 × 1m shares) + synergy of $0.1m (already post-tax) = **$1.70m.**

Total entity value is therefore $1.70m × 25 = **$42.5m.**

The number of shares post acquisition will be 2m (Blemish Co pre-acquisition) plus 0.5m new shares (1/2 × 1m) = **2.5m.**

The likely post-acquisition share price will therefore be **$17** ($42.5m / 2.5m).

This means that Dry Co is being offered one share worth $17 for two existing shares, ie **$8.50 per share.**

This is an attractive price because it is well above its current share price.

Comments on incorrect answers:

If you calculate the answer as $17 then you have calculated the post-acquisition price correctly but this was not what was asked for here.

The other answers are possible if you have forgotten to adjust the 1m Dry Co shares to reflect the fact that post acquisition these will be replaced by 0.5m Blemish Co shares.

52   The correct answer is: **$10.0m of equity/$2m debt/$20m convertible preference shares.**

The management team require $32m of finance.

The venture capitalist would not want to overload the company with debt so gearing would be minimised as is normal (we are told) in this industry.

The use of convertible preference shares give a greater certainty of some returns for the venture capitalist and the ability to convert into ordinary shares if the company is listed in future.

53   The correct answer is: **$3.96.**

Post-acquisition value:

200m × $8 = $800 million

100m × £1.50 = $150 million

PV Synergy = $40 million

800 + 150 + 40 = $990 million

Number of shares post-acquisition:

Current number of shares in A = 200 million

New shares issued = 100/2 × 1 = 50 million

Total number of shares = 200 + 50 = 250 million

Post-acquisition share price = $990/250 = $3.96

Incorrect answers:

Forgetting to add the synergy:

$950 million/250 million = $3.80

Incorrectly adding the shares of Company A and B:

$990million/(100m + 200m) = $3.30

Accounting for the share issue the wrong way round:

100m/1 × 2 new shares = 200m new shares + 200m existing shares = 400 million

$990 million/400 million = $2.48

54   The correct answer is: **$2.67**

Using M&M's formula for business valuations:

$V_g = V_u + T_B$

Currently Asparagus is a geared company with a total value of $100m of equity (40m × $2.5) plus $50m of debt so V_g = $150m.

From this we can identify V_u:

$150m = V_u + 0.2 × 50m$

$V_u = 150m - 10m = 140m$

The new loan will be for 25% of $100m = $25m.

Now we can value the company at its new level of gearing:

$V_g = V_u + T_B$

$V_g = 140m + 0.2 (50m + 25m)$

$V_g = 140 + 15 = $155m$

This is the value of the **entity** (debt + equity), and we know that the debt = $75m so the value of the equity = $155m - $75m = $80m.

This is the total value of the equity, to obtain the value of a share we need to divide by the number of shares. Before the share repurchase there were 40m shares, but after the share repurchase there are 25% less, ie 40 x 0.75 = 30m shares.

So the share price = $80 / 30m = **$2.67.**

55   The correct answer is: **Management accounts from the current owners showing the profits of the entity being bought for the past two years.**

The past profitability of the MBO will be influenced by its past strategy and also by overheads charged from Head Office.

The venture capitalist will be much more concerned about the future, and so key considerations will be: who is managing the entity, and what is the growth potential of the entity.

The only relevance of past profitability will be to assess the reasonableness of the cash flow projections; the reasonableness of the cash flow projections will be a part of the cash flow forecast.

56   The correct answer is: **£1 = $1.5294**

Future exchange rate = 1.5000 × (1 + 0.04/1 + 0.02)

57   The correct answer is: **The cost of an interest rate floor is higher than the cost of an interest rate collar.**

An interest rate floor requires the payment of a premium. A collar involves a combination of paying and receiving a premium and is therefore cheaper.

Incorrect answers:

An interest rate floor can be used to hedge an expected increase in interest rates. – a floor is an option which sets a lower amount to interest rates.

The premium on an interest rate option is payable when it is exercised – the premium is payable upfront.

The standardised nature of interest rate futures means that over- and under-hedging can be avoided.

Over- and under-hedging is inevitable due to the standardised nature of futures contracts.

58   The correct answer is: **$5,000**

The FRA effectively fixes the interest at the upper end of the spread of 3.2%.

The total interest charge is therefore

$10m × 3.2% × 3/12 = $80,000

The actual interest charge on the variable-rate loan is

$10m × 3% × 3/12 = $75,000

Therefore, the payment to the financial institution will be the difference of

$80,000 – $75,000 = $5,000

59   The correct answer is: **$248,781**

Money market hedge:

Expected receipt after six months = €500,000

Euro interest rate over six months = 5%/2 = 2.5%

Euros to borrow now in order to have €500,000 liability after six months = €500,000/1.025 = €487,805

Spot rate for selling euros today = 2 euro/$

Dollar deposit from borrowed euros at spot rate = 487,805/2 = $243,903

Dollar deposit rate over six months = 4%/2 = 2%

Value of the dollar deposit in six months' time = $243,903 × 1.02 = $248,781

60   The correct answer is: **$2,312.**

The forward rate for the euro is 0.8500–0.8650 to the $.

The rate for buying dollars (selling euros) will be the more expensive/higher rate. Converting into $s will result in there being more dollars than euros. So 2,000/0.8650 = $2,312.

The other answers are a result of using the wrong side of the spread and/or multiplying by the forward rate.

Pass:

70% to 100%

Well done, you have passed!

Fail:

0% to 69%

Unfortunately you have not passed.

Mathematical tables and exam formulae

Formulae and maths tables

Formulae

DVM

$$P_0 = \frac{d_1}{K_e - g}$$

$$K_e = \frac{d_1}{P_0} + g$$

$$g = r \times b$$

CAPM

$$k = R_f + [R_m - R_f]\beta$$

$$\beta_{eu} = \beta_{eg}\left[\frac{V_E}{V_E = V_D[1-t]}\right] + \beta_d\left[\frac{V_D[1-t]}{V_E = V_D[1-t]}\right]$$

$$\beta_{eg} = \beta_{eu} + [\beta_{eu} - \beta_d]\left[\frac{V_D[1-t]}{V_E}\right]$$

WACC

$$WACC = k_{eg}\left[\frac{V_E}{V_E + V_D}\right] + k_d[1-t]\left[\frac{V_D}{V_E + V_D}\right]$$

M&M

$$V_g = V_u + TB$$

$$k_{eg} = k_{eu} + [k_{eu} - k_d]\left[\frac{V_D[1-t]}{V_E}\right]$$

$$WACC = k_{eu}\left[1 - \left[\frac{V_D t}{V_E + V_D}\right]\right]$$

FX, interest rates & inflation

$$F_0 = S_0 \times \frac{[1 + r\,var]}{[1 + r\,base]}$$

$$S_1 = S_0 \times \frac{[1 + r\,var]}{[1 + r\,base]}$$

$$(1 + r_{nominal} = (1 + r_{real}) \times (1 + inflation))$$

TERP

$$TERP = \frac{1}{N+1}[(N \times cum\ rights\ price) + issue\ price]$$

$$Yield - adjusted\ TERP = \frac{1}{N+1}[(N \times cum\ rights\ price) + issue\ price \times (Y_{new} / Y_{old})]$$

VaR

VaR = confidence interval value × standard deviation

The confidence interval value comes from the normal distribution table.

Present value table

Present value of $1, that is $(1+r)^{-n}$ where r = interest rate; n = number of periods until payment or receipt.

Periods (n)	Interest rates (r)									
	1%	2%	3%	4%	5%	6%	7%	8%	9%	10%
1	0.990	0.980	0.971	0.962	0.952	0.943	0.935	0.926	0.917	0.909
2	0.980	0.961	0.943	0.925	0.907	0.890	0.873	0.857	0.842	0.826
3	0.971	0.942	0.915	0.889	0.864	0.840	0.816	0.794	0.772	0.751
4	0.961	0.924	0.888	0.855	0.823	0.792	0.763	0.735	0.708	0.683
5	0.951	0.906	0.863	0.822	0.784	0.747	0.713	0.681	0.650	0.621
6	0.942	0.888	0.837	0.790	0.746	0.705	0.666	0.630	0.596	0.564
7	0.933	0.871	0.813	0.760	0.711	0.665	0.623	0.583	0.547	0.513
8	0.923	0.853	0.789	0.731	0.677	0.627	0.582	0.540	0.502	0.467
9	0.914	0.837	0.766	0.703	0.645	0.592	0.544	0.500	0.460	0.424
10	0.905	0.820	0.744	0.676	0.614	0.558	0.508	0.463	0.422	0.386
11	0.896	0.804	0.722	0.650	0.585	0.527	0.475	0.429	0.388	0.350
12	0.887	0.788	0.701	0.625	0.557	0.497	0.444	0.397	0.356	0.319
13	0.879	0.773	0.681	0.601	0.530	0.469	0.415	0.368	0.326	0.290
14	0.870	0.758	0.661	0.577	0.505	0.442	0.388	0.340	0.299	0.263
15	0.861	0.743	0.642	0.555	0.481	0.417	0.362	0.315	0.275	0.239
16	0.853	0.728	0.623	0.534	0.458	0.394	0.339	0.292	0.252	0.218
17	0.844	0.714	0.605	0.513	0.436	0.371	0.317	0.270	0.231	0.198
18	0.836	0.700	0.587	0.494	0.416	0.350	0.296	0.250	0.212	0.180
19	0.828	0.686	0.570	0.475	0.396	0.331	0.277	0.232	0.194	0.164
20	0.820	0.673	0.554	0.456	0.377	0.312	0.258	0.215	0.178	0.149

Periods (n)	Interest rates (r)									
	11%	12%	13%	14%	15%	16%	17%	18%	19%	20%
1	0.901	0.893	0.885	0.877	0.870	0.862	0.855	0.847	0.840	0.833
2	0.812	0.797	0.783	0.769	0.756	0.743	0.731	0.718	0.706	0.694
3	0.731	0.712	0.693	0.675	0.658	0.641	0.624	0.609	0.593	0.579
4	0.659	0.636	0.613	0.592	0.572	0.552	0.534	0.516	0.499	0.482
5	0.593	0.567	0.543	0.519	0.497	0.476	0.456	0.437	0.419	0.402
6	0.535	0.507	0.480	0.456	0.432	0.410	0.390	0.370	0.352	0.335
7	0.482	0.452	0.425	0.400	0.376	0.354	0.333	0.314	0.296	0.279
8	0.434	0.404	0.376	0.351	0.327	0.305	0.285	0.266	0.249	0.233
9	0.391	0.361	0.333	0.308	0.284	0.263	0.243	0.225	0.209	0.194
10	0.352	0.322	0.295	0.270	0.247	0.227	0.208	0.191	0.176	0.162
11	0.317	0.287	0.261	0.237	0.215	0.195	0.178	0.162	0.148	0.135
12	0.286	0.257	0.231	0.208	0.187	0.168	0.152	0.137	0.124	0.112
13	0.258	0.229	0.204	0.182	0.163	0.145	0.130	0.116	0.104	0.093
14	0.232	0.205	0.181	0.160	0.141	0.125	0.111	0.099	0.088	0.078
15	0.209	0.183	0.160	0.140	0.123	0.108	0.095	0.084	0.079	0.065
16	0.188	0.163	0.141	0.123	0.107	0.093	0.081	0.071	0.062	0.054
17	0.170	0.146	0.125	0.108	0.093	0.080	0.069	0.060	0.052	0.045
18	0.153	0.130	0.111	0.095	0.081	0.069	0.059	0.051	0.044	0.038
19	0.138	0.116	0.098	0.083	0.070	0.060	0.051	0.043	0.037	0.031
20	0.124	0.104	0.087	0.073	0.061	0.051	0.043	0.037	0.031	0.026

Cumulative present value table

Cumulative present value of $1 per annum, Receivable or Payable at the end of each year
for n years $\dfrac{1-(1+r)^{-n}}{r}$

Periods (n)	Interest rates (r)									
	1%	2%	3%	4%	5%	6%	7%	8%	9%	10%
1	0.990	0.980	0.971	0.962	0.952	0.943	0.935	0.926	0.917	0.909
2	1.970	1.942	1.913	1.886	1.859	1.833	1.808	1.783	1.759	1.736
3	2.941	2.884	2.829	2.775	2.723	2.673	2.624	2.577	2.531	2.487
4	3.902	3.808	3.717	3.630	3.546	3.465	3.387	3.312	3.240	3.170
5	4.853	4.713	4.580	4.452	4.329	4.212	4.100	3.993	3.890	3.791
6	5.795	5.601	5.417	5.242	5.076	4.917	4.767	4.623	4.486	4.355
7	6.728	6.472	6.230	6.002	5.786	5.582	5.389	5.206	5.033	4.868
8	7.652	7.325	7.020	6.733	6.463	6.210	5.971	5.747	5.535	5.335
9	8.566	8.162	7.786	7.435	7.108	6.802	6.515	6.247	5.995	5.759
10	9.471	8.983	8.530	8.111	7.722	7.360	7.024	6.710	6.418	6.145
11	10.368	9.787	9.253	8.760	8.306	7.887	7.499	7.139	6.805	6.495
12	11.255	10.575	9.954	9.385	8.863	8.384	7.943	7.536	7.161	6.814
13	12.134	11.348	10.635	9.986	9.394	8.853	8.358	7.904	7.487	7.103
14	13.004	12.106	11.296	10.563	9.899	9.295	8.745	8.244	7.786	7.367
15	13.865	12.849	11.938	11.118	10.380	9.712	9.108	8.559	8.061	7.606
16	14.718	13.578	12.561	11.652	10.838	10.106	9.447	8.851	8.313	7.824
17	15.562	14.292	13.166	12.166	11.274	10.477	9.763	9.122	8.544	8.022
18	16.398	14.992	13.754	12.659	11.690	10.828	10.059	9.372	8.756	8.201
19	17.226	15.679	14.324	13.134	12.085	11.158	10.336	9.604	8.950	8.365
20	18.046	16.351	14.878	13.590	12.462	11.470	10.594	9.818	9.129	8.514

Periods (n)	Interest rates (r)									
	11%	12%	13%	14%	15%	16%	17%	18%	19%	20%
1	0.901	0.893	0.885	0.877	0.870	0.862	0.855	0.847	0.840	0.833
2	1.713	1.690	1.668	1.647	1.626	1.605	1.585	1.566	1.547	1.528
3	2.444	2.402	2.361	2.322	2.283	2.246	2.210	2.174	2.140	2.106
4	3.102	3.037	2.974	2.914	2.855	2.798	2.743	2.690	2.639	2.589
5	3.696	3.605	3.517	3.433	3.352	3.274	3.199	3.127	3.058	2.991
6	4.231	4.111	3.998	3.889	3.784	3.685	3.589	3.498	3.410	3.326
7	4.712	4.564	4.423	4.288	4.160	4.039	3.922	3.812	3.706	3.605
8	5.146	4.968	4.799	4.639	4.487	4.344	4.207	4.078	3.954	3.837
9	5.537	5.328	5.132	4.946	4.772	4.607	4.451	4.303	4.163	4.031
10	5.889	5.650	5.426	5.216	5.019	4.833	4.659	4.494	4.339	4.192
11	6.207	5.938	5.687	5.453	5.234	5.029	4.836	4.656	4.486	4.327
12	6.492	6.194	5.918	5.660	5.421	5.197	4.988	4.793	4.611	4.439
13	6.750	6.424	6.122	5.842	5.583	5.342	5.118	4.910	4.715	4.533
14	6.982	6.628	6.302	6.002	5.724	5.468	5.229	5.008	4.802	4.611
15	7.191	6.811	6.462	6.142	5.847		5.324	5.092	4.876	4.675
16	7.379	6.974	6.604	6.265	5.954	5.668	5.405	5.162	4.938	4.730
17	7.549	7.120	6.729	6.373	6.047	5.749	5.475	5.222	4.990	4.775
18	7.702	7.250	6.840	6.467	6.128	5.818	5.534	5.273	5.033	4.812
19	7.839	7.366	6.938	6.550	6.198	5.877	5.584	5.316	5.070	4.843
20	7.963	7.469	7.025	6.623	6.259	5.929	5.628	5.353	5.101	4.870

Normal distribution table

This table gives the area under the normal curve between the mean and a point Z standard deviations above the mean. The corresponding area for deviations below the mean can be found by symmetry.

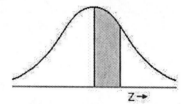

$Z = \frac{(x-\mu)}{\sigma}$	0.00	0.01	0.02	0.03	0.04	0.05	0.06	0.07	0.08	0.09
0.0	.0000	.0040	.0080	.0120	.0159	.0199	.0239	.0279	.0319	.0359
0.1	.0398	.0438	.0478	.0517	.0557	.0596	.0636	.0675	.0714	.0753
0.2	.0793	.0832	.0871	.0910	.0948	.0987	.1026	.1064	.1103	.1141
0.3	.1179	.1217	.1255	.1293	.1331	.1368	.1406	.1443	.1480	.1517
0.4	.1554	.1591	.1628	.1664	.1700	.1736	.1772	.1808	.1844	.1879
0.5	.1915	.1950	.1985	.2019	.2054	.2088	.2123	.2157	.2190	.2224
0.6	.2257	.2291	.2324	.2357	.2389	.2422	.2454	.2486	.2518	.2549
0.7	.2580	.2611	.2642	.2673	.2704	.2734	.2764	.2794	.2823	.2852
0.8	.2881	.2910	.2939	.2967	.2995	.3023	.3051	.3078	.3106	.3133
0.9	.3159	.3186	.3212	.3238	.3264	.3289	.3315	.3340	.3365	.3389
1.0	.3413	.3438	.3461	.3485	.3508	.3531	.3554	.3577	.3599	.3621
1.1	.3643	.3665	.3686	.3708	.3729	.3749	.3770	.3790	.3810	.3830
1.2	.3849	.3869	.3888	.3907	.3925	.3944	.3962	.3980	.3997	.4015
1.3	.4032	.4049	.4066	.4082	.4099	.4115	.4131	.4147	.4162	.4177
1.4	.4192	.4207	.4222	.4236	.4251	.4265	.4279	.4292	.4306	.4319
1.5	.4332	.4345	.4357	.4370	.4382	.4394	.4406	.4418	.4430	.4441
1.6	.4452	.4463	.4474	.4485	.4495	.4505	.4515	.4525	.4535	.4545
1.7	.4554	.4564	.4573	.4582	.4591	.4599	.4608	.4616	.4625	.4633
1.8	.4641	.4649	.4656	.4664	.4671	.4678	.4686	.4693	.4699	.4706
1.9	.4713	.4719	.4726	.4732	.4738	.4744	.4750	.4756	.4762	.4767
2.0	.4772	.4778	.4783	.4788	.4793	.4798	.4803	.4808	.4812	.4817
2.1	.4821	.4826	.4830	.4834	.4838	.4842	.4846	.4850	.4854	.4857
2.2	.4861	.4865	.4868	.4871	.4875	.4878	.4881	.4884	.4887	.4890
2.3	.4893	.4896	.4898	.4901	.4904	.4906	.4909	.4911	.4913	.4916
2.4	.4918	.4920	.4922	.4925	.4927	.4929	.4931	.4932	.4934	.4936
2.5	.4938	.4940	.4941	.4943	.4945	.4946	.4948	.4949	.4951	.4952
2.6	.4953	.4955	.4956	.4957	.4959	.4960	.4961	.4962	.4963	.4964
2.7	.4965	.4966	.4967	.4968	.4969	.4970	.4971	.4972	.4973	.4974
2.8	.4974	.4975	.4976	.4977	.4977	.4978	.4979	.4980	.4980	.4981
2.9	.4981	.4982	.4983	.4983	.4984	.4984	.4985	.4985	.4986	.4986
3.0	.4987	.4987	.4987	.4988	.4988	.4989	.4989	.4989	.4990	.4990
3.1	.4990	.4991	.4991	.4991	.4992	.4992	.4992	.4992	.4993	.4993
3.2	.4993	.4993	.4994	.4994	.4994	.4994	.4994	.4995	.4995	.4995
3.3	.4995	.4995	.4995	.4996	.4996	.4996	.4996	.4996	.4996	.4997
3.4	.4997	.4997	.4997	.4997	.4997	.4997	.4997	.4997	.4997	.4998

Notes